THE IDEAL CITY

Vision of the Celestial Jerusalem; from *Liber Floridus*, Ghent.
(By courtesy of the University Library, Ghent)

The Ideal City

ITS ARCHITECTURAL EVOLUTION

Helen Rosenau

ICON EDITIONS

HARPER & ROW, Publishers

New York, Evanston, San Francisco, London

TO ADAM ZVI

FIRST U.S. EDITION

SBN: 06-438461-6 (cloth); 06-430015-3 (paperback)

LIBRARY OF CONGRESS CATALOG CARD NUMBER: 74-188931

CONTENTS

LIST OF ILLUSTRATIONS

ABBREVIATIONS

Boullée   H. Rosenau, *Boullée's Treatise on Architecture*, London 1953.

Hautecœur   L. Hautecœur, *Histoire de l'architecture classique en France*, Paris 1943, etc.
        I.   *La Formation de l'idéal classique – La Renaissance*, 1943.
        IV. *Seconde moitié du 18e siècle – Le Style Louis XVI*, 1952.
        V. *Révolution et Empire*, 1953.

Lavedan   P. Lavedan, *Histoire de l'urbanisme*, Paris 1926, etc.
        I.   *Antiquité – Moyen Age*, 1926.
        II.   *Renaissance et temps modernes*, 1941.
        III. *Époque contemporaine*, 1952.

Ledoux   C.-N. Ledoux, *L'Architecture considérée sous le rapport de l'art, des mœurs et de la législation*, Paris 1804–46.

Prieur   *Collection des Prix que la ci-devant Académie d'Architecture proposoit et couronnoit tous les ans*, 1787–96. Engravings by Prieur and van Cléemputte. This work has been edited by H. Rosenau in *Architectural History, Journal of the Society of Architectural Historians of Great Britain*, Vol. III, 1960, p. 17 ff.

Projets   Allais, Détournelle and Vaudoyer; *Grands Prix d'architecture, projets couronnés par l'Académie d'Architecture et l'Institut de France*, Paris 1806.

R.I.B.A.   Royal Institute of British Architects.

Social Purpose   H. Rosenau, *Social Purpose in Architecture*, London 1971.

Thieme-Becker   U. Thieme and F. Becker, *Allgemeines Lexicon der Bildenden Künstler*, Leipzig 1907, etc.

Pauly-Wissowa   *Pauly's Real-Encyclopädie*, new edition by G. Wissowa, Stuttgart 1894, etc.

ACKNOWLEDGEMENTS

First Edition

The publication of books presupposes a good deal of collective labour, and the present one cannot claim to provide an exception. It is impossible to thank all those who in one way or another have helped in the completion of this study. First I would like to record my deep appreciation of Sir William Holford's stimulating and encouraging Preface [to the first edition]. I wish to take the opportunity of expressing my gratitude to the Staff of the Library of the British Museum, to Mr J. C. Palmes, the Librarian and the Staff of the Royal Institute of British Architects, to the Keeper and the Staff of the Library of the Victoria and Albert Museum, to Dr K. Martin, the then Director of the Badisches Landesmuseum, and Dr L. Fischel for assistance in Karlsruhe, to Professor Middeldorf of the German Institute of the History of Art in Florence, to Professor Heydenreich and Dr Lehmann Brockhaus of the Central Institute of the History of Art in Munich, and to Mr A. C. Sewter, the Head of the History of Art Department, and Professor Vinaver of the University of Manchester.

Miss Jean Barrie, Miss Vera Douie, the Librarian of the Fawcett Library, London, Miss V. F. Forrest, Mr L. B. Keeble, Senior Lecturer and Director of Studies in the Town Planning Department of University College, London, and Mrs Valerie Martin-Romaya, have made valuable suggestions. I would especially like to thank Mrs Ilse Barasch, who helped in the compilation of the Index.

Mr S. Kadleigh has allowed the reproduction of some of his designs for High Paddington; the Reconstruction Department of the City of Rotterdam, through the intermediary of Miss J. Swankhuisen, has supplied photographs and valuable information on the architectural progress of that city. Sir John Summerson gave permission to study works in the Sir John Soane's Museum; M. J. Porchet and the Staffs of the Cabinet des Estampes of the Bibliothèque Nationale, Paris, the John Rylands Library, the History of Art Department and the Library of the University of Manchester, provided photographs and facilities for study.

I wish to express to Mr A. W. Wheen my personal sense of gratitude for his assistance in the revision of the text and his constant encouragement and understanding. Michael A. M. B. Carmi has shown, despite his youth, an unswerving loyalty and sustained interest in the progress of this work, and I wish to take the opportunity of recording my fullest appreciation.

H. R.

London, 1959

Second Edition

The present edition is an attempt to bring my study of *The Ideal City* up to date without encumbering the book with too many additions and annotations. Nevertheless, some new material has been incorporated, and it is hoped that this will demonstrate some typical and relevant facts.

It is my pleasant duty to add my thanks to Dr D. E. Rhodes and Mr I. R. Willison and the Staff of the British Museum Library, Mr Peter Slater and the Staff of the slide collection of the University of London Library, Mr David Dean, the Librarian and the Staff of the Royal Institute of British Architects, Mr Jean Adhémar of the Cabinet des Estampes at the Bibliotèque Nationale, Paris, and the Staff of the print room at the Library of Congress in Washington.

On a personal level, I wish to thank Michael and Louise Carmi for their help in this revised version and Mr Dennis Sharp for his continuous interest, Mr S. G. Pembroke and Miss Elisabeth Hobley for a number of valuable suggestions; Mr K. E. Wilson for his help with proof reading, and Celia Phillips, Elizabeth Kingsley-Rowe, Jenny Towndrow and John Leath for their care in the preparation of this book.

H. R.
London, 1972

FOREWORD

A Citie is a perfect and absolute assembly or communion of many townes or streets in one.

(Aristotle's *Politics*, translation of 1598)

The desire to attain a perfect physical environment and a more satisfying way of life is characteristic of Western European civilization, since it possesses dynamic force and incorporates economic and social change and experiment. It presupposes emphasis on freedom, and a willingness to strive for progress. The field of this enquiry is confined to these main European trends, not because it is unrewarding to roam further afield, but because developments and conditions outside this area are of a different character, and would require detailed studies of their own.

Planning, rigid and static in the early civilizations of the Middle East, became more varied and dynamic in the Hellenistic and Roman Empires, and after an interlude during the Middle Ages, gained in significance during the Renaissance and the Baroque periods. In the Age of Enlightenment, the change in emphasis from religious to social considerations led to the emergence of a markedly secular epoch[1]; it is from this that the contemporary period is derived. How European developments will change in the future cannot be discussed profitably in the present study. It is past evolution, not prophecy, which is its subject.

It should be understood that the survey attempted here cannot, by its very nature, be comprehensive. It is meant to illustrate the broad outline of an evolution, which, whilst historically interesting, may also include suggestions for the contemporary and future planner.

The selection of illustrations is based mainly on individual merit, but is equally meant to illuminate collective trends, and thus deal with the evolution of types. It is inevitable that material should be scanty for the earlier periods, especially as documentation is rare in so specialized a field as town-planning. Here the task is mainly one of reconstruction, while for the later epochs a substantial documentation exists, from which relevant examples have to be selected. An attempt will be made to concentrate on the most significant and telling designs and their interpretation.

The term 'city' is applied to important communities and centres of population which represent traits similar to, or derived from, the *civitas*. Thus, for example, monasteries – in the Middle Ages – and Owen's 'Villages of Unity and Mutual Co-operation' will be included.

Since changing social conditions mould the vision of artists as well as patrons, works of art are bound to reflect their period. On the other hand, a striving after the absolute is innate in man and finds expression not only in religion and philosophy, but also in art and architecture.[2] These considerations of the ideal may even affect the basic economic structure, as can be clearly seen in the development of town and country planning in England; for example, the concept of the garden city is remarkably wasteful for a small and overcrowded island and cannot be explained by economic preoccupations alone. Or, to put it in a different manner, as expressed by Friedrich Engels: 'The superstructure influences the base'. In this instance sociological and ideological reasons act as more powerful agents than purely materialistic considerations.[3]

For the purpose of this study an ideal city represents a religious vision, or a secular view, in which social consciousness of the needs of the population is allied with a harmonious conception of artistic unity. That an ideal plan, when executed, generates its own problems through changing circumstances hardly needs stressing, but its value remains unaffected as far as it is a projection of a perfect image, a vivid expression of optimistic faith; indeed, this is perhaps the most striking feature the ideal images have in common: they are based on a belief in betterment, either on this earth or in the hereafter. They illuminate an attitude emphasizing not only personal happiness, but the overriding significance of the communal or community factors, for their own as well as for the individual's sake. Ideal images emerged in periods of social change, such as the early Renaissance or the Age of Enlightenment, when the breaking up of an older economic order facilitated cultural experimentation.

The ideal plan refers to the site as a unity and expresses the aspirations rather than the achievements of any particular civilization; it is intended for, and applicable to, varying circumstances. Its alternative is the working drawing, destined for one particular place and purpose. The image of the ideal city thus seeks the universal answer to temporary problems, and by so doing reflects as well as challenges its social background.

This study does not deal with the destruction or the preservation of existing buildings, neither does it imply that the development of parts of towns is valueless. It emphasizes the architectural and social unity of the city, a unity which, spreading from the centre, may even redeem the sprawling suburbs of the present day. For this reason, partial plans will be included in exceptional cases, if they are of significance for the urban life of the community as a whole.

If special emphasis is given to France, this is due to her pre-eminence in matters artistic as far as continuity of evolution is concerned. While other European nations have come to the fore in particular periods, France has, as it were, continuously been the conscience of Europe so far as the general level of taste is concerned. French artists, even if less than outstanding, have therefore been able to reach a high level of attainment, so that evolution in France has been in the past less dependent on individual contributions than that of other European countries, for example Germany. This is particularly true of the late 18th century, the period of Enlightenment, when the vision of a perfect environment has been realized in designs of great clarity and of optimistic affirmation.

The concept of the ideal city raises the problem of freedom of will rising above sociological and biological limitations. The answer, by necessity, has to be one of individual belief, rather than factual proof. At any rate, the consistent striving for perfection is a clear indication of the recurrent human desire to attain a state in which conditioned necessity is replaced by liberty and harmony.[4]

Although this work is not a sociological study, it is hoped that the plans and designs assembled here will prove of interest to the sociologist, and will add to the elucidation of sociological processes.[5] The psychologist may also be concerned with the significance of ideal planning, since this cogently illustrates the growth of 'social interest', as described by Alfred Adler.[6] Furthermore, the *mandala*, the circular plan, is a basic psychological factor in the theory of C. G. Jung.[7] His concept of the integration of the personality by developing the 'inferior function' is also helpful in assessing the contribution of the visionary planners: they emphasize neglected cultural tendencies, and give answers to problems, which, although collectively experienced, are nevertheless not consciously realized. Thus the Heavenly Jerusalem was a projection of harmony, seen against the strife of the Middle Ages, and the evolution of capitalism was the background for the vision of the classless society which sustained the planners of the Age of Enlightenment and the Utopian Socialists. Since works of art transcend their social situation, there exists a frequent time-lag between artistic creation and popular appreciation; in a wider sense, this was one of the underlying causes of the phenomenon of revival or Renaissance, the renewed interest in, and understanding of, the art of the past.

At the present time the unconscious factors in artistic creation are frequently overrated, so it is perhaps as well to bear in mind that the planners of ideal cities did not reflect ambiguous 'archetypes' in the Jungian sense, archetypes which, by their very nature, constitute polarities.[8] These designs express a different tendency – the emphasis on the conscious contribution towards redemption or social betterment – and serve, therefore, the conception of progress; this naturally does not imply that in fact every planner's subjective views were progressive or achieved realization. Nevertheless, their images of ideal cities can act as regulative models rather than as precepts for everyday life.[9] At the same time, they meant to express universal or typical tendencies, and for this reason the examples selected are not to be regarded as isolated, but as interpreting *multum in parvo*.

To sum up: the perennial theme of art is an intensified vision regarding the quality of life and therefore the subject of ideal cities reaches right into the core of artistic creation. It is the regularity of plan combined with a concern for a better society which characterizes and enhances ideal planning.

A word may be added on the presentation of the subject: a brief outline of historical evolution will be given according to the dominating styles. While the conventional divisions of art history have been made use of in this study, the writer is aware of their occasional arbitrariness and tendency to overlap. However, they do help to clarify the general trend of development, and for this reason cannot be easily dispensed with. Although it would have been tempting to study the designs in more detail, this temptation had to be resisted, since, for the purpose under discussion, it was the unity of development, rather than its ramifications, which counted. The selection of illustrations may be regarded as the underlying documentation, but they also form an independent part of the work and may be perused for their own sake. It is hoped that they will be of interest for their intrinsic value, as well as for their sequential relevance. The aim of this work is primarily to present designs and to let them speak for themselves. It can only be hoped that the searchlight thus trained on the past will in fact be revealing, and help towards a fuller understanding of architectural vision.[10]

---

1. Whether, in order to explain this change, the main emphasis has to be placed on economic or ideological considerations cannot be made the object of this study. On the desire for progress, cf. R. V. Sampson, *The Idea of Progress in the 18th Century*, London 1957.

2. H. Read, *Icon and Idea*, London 1955. On the problems of symmetry, cf. L. L. Whyte, *Aspects of Form*, London 1951, and H. Weyl, *Symmetry*, Princeton 1952. For contrasting aesthetic values, cf. Chr. Hussey, *The Picturesque*, London 1927, 2nd ed., London 1967.

3. *The Correspondence of K. Marx and F. Engels*, 1934 ed., pp. 475 ff. and 561 ff. M. Adler, *Engels als Denker*, 2nd ed., Berlin 1925.

4. K. R. Popper, *The Open Society and its Enemies*, 2nd ed., London 1952.

5. M. Weber, *Gesammelte Aufsätze zur Religionssoziologie*, Tübingen 1920–21, is methodologically important for our purpose, although it deals with abstract concepts rather than with factual surveys.

6. A. Adler, *Social Interest*, London 1938.

7. C. G. Jung, *Memories, Dreams, Reflections*, ed. A. Jaffé, London 1967, *Psychological Types*, London 1923, and many of his later works. The complete English edition is being published by Routledge and Kegan Paul.

8. The contributions of S. Freud and C. G. Jung, although valid in their own spheres, fail to emphasize those aspects of artistic creation which escape an assessment based on mainly unconscious motivations.

9. cf. especially among L. Mumford's numerous and influential publications: *The Culture of Cities* and *Technics and Civilization*, London 1938 and 1934 respectively.

10. Lavedan is still invaluable for a broad survey of the history of town-planning.

Part One

I

The Greek Tradition

In order to survey the development of ideal planning in Western Europe it is necessary to consider briefly the ancient traditions upon which this evolution is based. As the late Professor Frankfort cogently pointed out in his book on *The Art and Architecture of the Ancient Orient,* in Ur 'the temples and palaces were the only buildings with aesthetic pretensions'.[1] It is furthermore true to say that the planners in the Orient concentrated on such buildings, whilst the dwellings of the less fortunate members of the community were treated with scant attention. The Assyrian proverb,

> The man is the shadow of the god
> The slave is the shadow of the man
> But the king is god.

Clay tablet of *c.* 600 B.C. depicting the regions of the world. (By courtesy of the British Museum)

epitomizes a static view of civilization,[2] in which palaces and ziggurats with their precincts were regarded as representations of, and substitutes for, cosmic relationships, the underlying basic pattern of planning being the square. It is against this background that the novel developments of the Greek, Roman and Jewish concepts of the ideal city have to be set. On the other hand, the circular form is not entirely absent. It occurs in a small Babylonian clay tablet, depicting the regions of the world, and also in a relief from Nineveh, showing four domestic occupations in the subdivisions of a fortified encampment (both of which are in the British Museum).[3] The latter seems reminiscent of the Biblical story (Genesis XL) regarding the functions and dignity of Pharaoh's Butler and Baker.

It is in classical Greece with its City States, and in the Hellenistic and Roman Empires, that a significant and gradual change in overall planning took place, although the early stages of these developments are still largely unknown, pending the unforeseeable results of future excavations. Admirers of the suggestive and unplanned effect of the Acropolis in Athens may well differ in their taste from the contemporaries of Plato, who in the Fifth Book of his treatise on *Laws* demanded a city as near as possible to the centre of the country, an acropolis circled by a ring wall. Plato divided his ideal town into 12 parts,

planned for 5,040 plots, each of which was to be subdivided
to allow for the equalization of the quality of land, the same
citizen receiving a superior central portion and an inferior one
at the periphery. The 5,000 individual households were to
nominate one son as heir, or, if no son was alive, the husband
of a daughter; and surplus children were to be distributed by
adoption or emigration to ensure a static population.

Plato, *Laws*, V, 740 and XI, 923

In the *Timaeus* and *Critias* the ancient city of Athens is
characterized by various classes of inhabitant: the priests, the
artisans, the husbandmen and warriors. The separation of these
classes is mentioned in the former and presupposed in the
descriptions of the latter. It is likely that in these statements
Plato reflected and modernized ancient conceptions of static
and harmonious communities which were associated with the
abodes of the gods and the palaces of the kings.[4]

In the same works Plato also described the legendary island
of 'Atlantis', which contained a mount, encircled by five zones
of land and water, and a palace enclosed by round walls on the
'secret island', presumably an artificial subdivision of the larger

Relief from Nineveh, showing four
domestic occupations in a fortified
encampment. (By courtesy of the
British Museum)
[See p. 19.]

isle. There was a rectangular plain, divided into 60,000 plots, each of which was a square.

Thus the two basic mathematical forms, the square and the circle, are found in juxtaposition. These elements, seen universally in all civilizations, remained the *tracé régulateur*, in the sense in which Le Corbusier uses the term, right up to the contemporary period. The fact that Plato mentions the plain is significant, not only because of its regular form, but also because a planned environment is more easily realized in a flat region, whereas mountainous sites largely superimpose their own shape on the human matrix. On the other hand, hills and mountains and their protecting walls achieve the simplest type of strategic protection. For this reason a rudimentary form of circle appears in primitive civilizations, as also does a vaguely round or elliptic hut, in which angles are anxiously avoided. Such shapes only partially reflect the character and regularity of the true circle.

Plato's prototypes for the lay-out of Atlantis may be connected with pre-Hellenic fortifications in Greece, or the ring of walls encircling Mantincia in about 460 B.C.[5] Isolated central buildings, such as the Tholos of Epidaurus, reveal the circle as an aesthetic factor, but, from the evidence available, the same principle does not seem to have been applied consciously to town-planning. Hellenistic cities, when planned, belonged to the chequer-board type, as seen in Miletus, Priene, and also originally in the Piraeus, as built by Hippodamus of Miletus. From these facts it appears that Plato's sources were not observations regarding his environment, but sprang from traditions of a magical or cosmological nature; they are used in a formalized manner, expressing primarily aesthetic concepts of regularity and order, which in turn may well be indebted to the Pythagorean tradition.

The division regarding social stratification in the Second Book of Aristotle's *Politics* appears similar to that found in the *Timaeus* and *Critias*, and is attributed to the theories of the same Hippodamus of Miletus, who thus appears as a thinker as well as an architect.[6] Three classes – artisans, farmers and warriors – are described, and a fourth class of priests is presupposed, since the land is divided into three parts: sacred, public and private. In his turn, Aristophanes in *The Birds* was aware of the concept of circular geometric cities, when he poked fun at Plato, his disciples and the rigid planners. The combination – architect and planner – found in the person of Hippodamus was to become a characteristic feature in European evolution.

In an interesting article, Ivanka discusses the views attributed to Hippodamus in the *Politics*, since they form a separate part of the treatise, and may originally have belonged to a different work. Ivanka implies that the suggestions Aristotle made to

Alexander the Great for the planning of new towns were
rejected by the king, who, far from wanting to set up cities
in the Greek democratic tradition, wished to continue as an
autocratic ruler over his subjected peoples.[7] Aristotle favoured
moderation in size and was an advocate of the walled city, the
walls being not only an ornamental element, but also necessary
for defence. According to him, it was Hippodamus of Miletus
who favoured a fixed maximum size for the city state, which
was to comprise 10,000 people.

Aristotle used an ancient pattern of society, as preserved in
the *Critias*, and transformed it to serve his own political purpose.
But he failed to exert his influence, since Alexander attempted
to unify the various populations under his autocratic rule, thus
becoming the creator of the vast Hellenistic cities. However,
when the Grecian symbol of the *polis*, the goddess of Fortune,
Tyche, crowned by a circlet of walls and peacefully seated, was
associated with the newly created towns such as Alexandria and
Antioch, she still personified the tradition of the enclosed and
protective aspect of the city state.[8] The statue in the Vatican
Museum, representing the Tyche of Antioch by Eutychides of
Sicyon, is a marble copy of the bronze original and shows the
goddess, following the usual iconography, holding a sheaf of
corn. The river god Orontes is seen at her feet. The work is a
telling symbol of womanhood regarded as a protective and
bountiful force, allied to good fortune and the prosperity of the
city.

This type of representation was frequently found in monumental statues as well as on numerous coins, and its popularity
persisted in the Roman period. It is reflected in a medieval copy
of the *Tabula Peutingeriana*, a Christian adaptation of a road map
of the Roman world, now in the Vienna National Library.
Here the cities are shown in perspective, enclosed by their walls,
and smaller centres by foreshortened individual buildings or
groups. Antioch is represented by Tyche, seated, a halo round
her head, Orontes at her feet, whilst Roma, within her circular
walls, is enthroned holding up the orb, and Constantinople
is presumably characterized by the column of Constantine,
erected in A.D. 331. The feminine figures, which were originally
based on the prototype of the protecting city-goddess of
Hellenism, were altered to masculine ones during the medieval
period, showing how much their underlying meaning had been
misunderstood and forgotten.[9]

The Roman Tradition

The only extant treatise by a practising architect of the Roman
period is the work by Vitruvius, *De Architectura Libri Decem*,

Copy of *Tabula Peutingeriana* (detail).
National Library, Vienna. (Photograph:
Bildarchiv der Oesterreichischen Na-
tionalbibliothek)

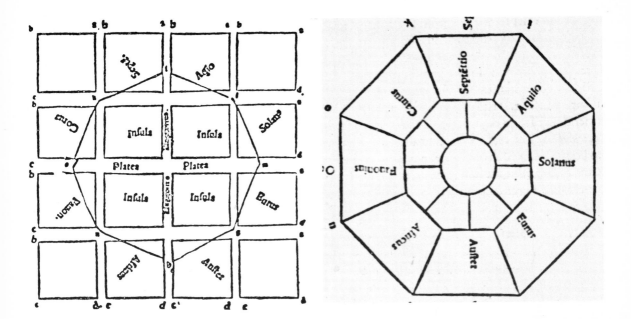

Vitruvius, Town Plans, from the edition
of 1511.

Vitruvius, Book I, 6-8

presumably belonging to the Augustan Age. Owing to the
author's lack of originality, for which posterity has cause to be
thankful, this remarkable document faithfully reflects the
dominant trends of its period. The emphasis is on architecture
for the rich and powerful, whilst the social question looms
in the background, hardly recognized as yet. Vitruvius's main
preoccupation is with formal and structural considerations: the
variety of the building programme, including civic structures,
is discussed in three sections dealing with sacred, public and
private buildings, a sensible arrangement which has been
almost universally followed by later writers. Vitruvius stipulated
that the market-place should be in the centre of the town, but
erected near the harbour in a sea-port. The examples enumer-
ated are of a predominantly practical nature; but when
Vitruvius deals with the town-plan as a whole he envisages an
ideal city.

The city was to be enclosed by a protecting circular wall,
reinforced by towers for strategic reasons. For hygienic purposes,
the eight streets dividing the sections were to avoid the radial
arrangement of the eight assumed directions of the prevailing
winds. Vitruvius was aware of the irregularity of the actual
winds, and thus added that further currents of air and breezes
existed, originating from local conditions. But in spite of that
knowledge, he respected an overriding geometric pattern. The
figure eight was traditional in myth and astrology: the Tower
of the Winds in Athens was dedicated to eight deities, and the
so-called 'Etruscan Bronze Liver' of the Library of Piacenza,
which was used in the rites of divination by the haruspices,

was divided into 16 parts, doubling the traditional figure. The meaning of these rites, although obscure in detail, emphasizes the relation between man and the universe, and it appears significant that Vitruvius's town is similarly divided by the directions of the eight winds and the streets located between them.

The ancient 'Terramare' settlements were not circular, but built in a chequer-board alignment, and even the round Etruscan tombs were arranged along roads in a loose manner, and did not follow a regular pattern.[10] It should also be remembered that the Roman *mundus* was of circular form, though it had no visible influence on the form of town planning. It is therefore clear that Vitruvius, like Plato, designed his ideal city not on the basis of actual surroundings, but to satisfy the concepts of harmony, regularity and enclosure by using a circular form. Nevertheless, the importance of the Platonic tradition in Vitruvius's work should not be overrated; although the philosopher is mentioned by name in rather a vague manner on a number of occasions, no exact borrowings are found. For example, the division of the city into eight or 16 compartments is a deviation from Plato, who favoured 12 divisions in his *Laws*. Vitruvius applies the natural division of

Forma Urbis Romae, fragments now in the Capitoline Museum, Rome.

the circle into multiples of four, whilst Plato's arrangement is reminiscent of the 12 subdivisions of the square, used in calculating the lunar year.[11]

In spite of the fact that many-storeyed buildings were common in the late Republican period of Rome, they are not mentioned in Vitruvius's text. This illustrates his lack of interest in the life of the common people. On the other hand, he discussed the arrangement of houses according to the wealth or the moderate means of the owners, and showed interest in farms and the requirements of the merchants. The fact that Vitruvius catered for the powerful and wealthy corroborates Rostovtzeff's theory that the cleavage between the higher and lower classes was a basic factor in the eventual decline of the Empire.[12] Vitruvius's ideal city is therefore no social Utopia, but a formal pattern, characteristic of his own period. His clear classification of designs into ground-plan, *ichnographia*, elevation, *orthographia*, and perspective view, *scaenographia*, had a lasting influence on medieval art.

Vitruvius, Book I, 2

One example of an executed ground-plan has survived from the Roman period, the *Forma Urbis Romae*, originally affixed to the wall of the Templum Sacrae Urbis after A.D. 203, now preserved in a fragmentary state in the Capitoline Museum. It attempts a comprehensive survey, omitting detail, yet the various sites are recognizable and individual buildings are clearly shown. The *Forma Urbis Romae* fulfilled a magical and religious function, by indicating the area over which Roma, the goddess of the city, wielded her protective powers. We gain from it a clear idea of the kind of design which exerted a formative influence on the early Middle Ages. Although now an isolated and unique work, it must originally have been one of many. Its preservation was undoubtedly due to its sacred character: had it been a working drawing, it would have been lost.[13]

The Jewish Tradition

As important as the formal Classical tradition is the Jewish subject matter which played a significant part in formulating the medieval conception of the ideal city. Originally based on Babylonian myths, the Jewish themes were developed in a spiritualized manner: they centred round the Temple and its site, the city of Jerusalem.

The Jewish Temple, with its hierarchy which led to the religious supremacy of Jerusalem, was represented on the coins of the Bar Kokba period, A.D. 132–5, and on the central panel of the second Synagogue in Dura-Europos of A.D. 245. It is shown as a Hellenistic building adorned by at least four pillars,

Panel above the niche, Dura-Europos Synagogue. Museum of Damascus. (Photo H. Pearson)

the opening in the former showing the Ark and in the latter a closed monumental doorway. The characteristic flat roof is based on Scripture and was retained in other and later representations of the building. Since the Temple stands for the idea of redemption and fulfilment, it was related to the conception of the Heavenly Jerusalem.[14]

2 Chronicles III, 4

The pattern of the Tabernacle, which, according to the Bible, was shown by God to Moses, represents a concept of ideal planning, especially as the location of the tribes with their tents forms part of the plan. The pictorial tradition is an ancient one, going back beyond the illustrations of the *Codex Amiatinus*. It still persists in Jacob Jehuda Leon 'Templo's' engravings of 1654.[15]

Exodus XXV, 9

Numbers II

In Ezekiel the Messianic Temple was expected to be located in the Holy City of Jerusalem, which it enhanced symbolically. A full description of the Temple and its precincts, its materials and measurements, as well as the adjoining districts, is given here. The Sanctuary, in the shape of a cube, is described in the first Book of Kings and in the second Book of Chronicles. This

Ezekiel XL–XLIII

1 Kings VI, 16–20
2 Chronicles III, 8

Ezekiel XLV, 2 and XLVIII, 16

basic geometric form expresses symbolically a universal meaning.[16] The square form of the Holy City in Ezekiel reflects the same concepts. Reference to the Heavenly City is also found in the twenty-first chapter of the Book of Revelation, in which its descent from Heaven, its high walls, and its 12 gates are described. The city is a cube, like the Sanctuary according to the first Book of Kings, and is ornamented with precious stones, symbolizing priceless value. C. P. S. Menon suggested that the square outline was based on ancient cosmological traditions which were largely influenced by mathematical considerations.[17] He also pointed out the basic similarity between Indian, Chinese and Near-Eastern views on this subject, implying an intercommunication between these ancient civilizations which transcended limitations of race and culture. These are too frequently forgotten when the significance of tribal memories and supposedly self-contained national cultures is stressed.

Engraving from Templo's *Retrato del Tabernaculo de Moseh*, Amsterdam 1654, showing the Tabernacle, its encampment, and the wagons of the Israelites carrying offerings.

In the words of the late Dr Paul Winter, 'The earliest

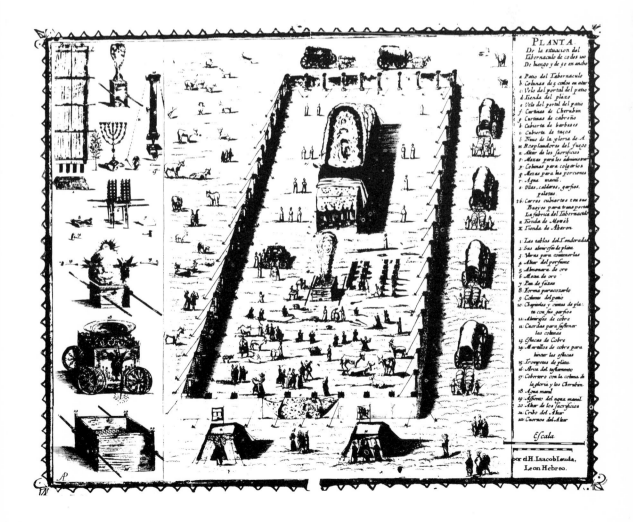

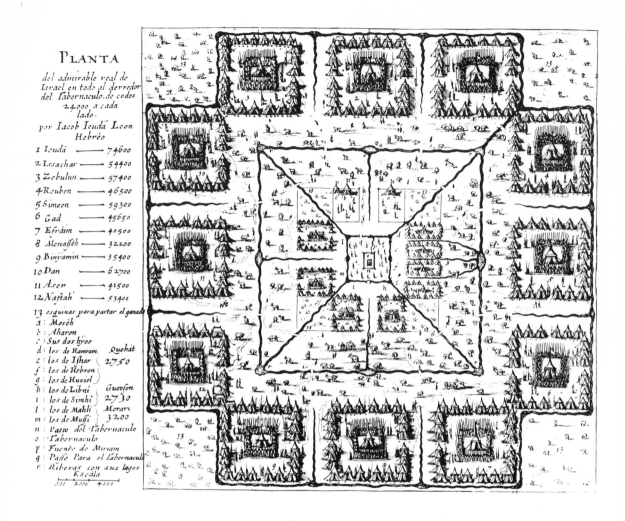

PLANTA

del admirable real de
Israel en todo al derredor
del Tabernaculo, de codos
24.000 a cada
lado

por Iacob Ieudá Leon
Hebréo

1 *Ieudá* ———— 74600
2 *Issachar* ——— 54400
3 *Zebulun* ——— 57400
4 *Rouben* ——— 46500
5 *Simeon* ——— 59300
6 *Gad* ———— 45650
7 *Efráim* ——— 40500
8 *Menasséh* —— 32200
9 *Binyamin* —— 35400
10 *Dan* ———— 62700
11 *Aser* ———— 41500
12 *Naftali* ——— 53400
13 *esquinas para pastar el ganado*
a : *Mosséh*
b : *Aharon*
c : *Sus dos hyos*
d : *los de Hamram* ⎫ *Quehát*
e : *los de Ishar* ⎬ 2750
f : *los de Hebron* ⎪
g : *los de Huziel* ⎭
h : *los de Libni* ⎫ *Guersón*
i : *los de Simhi* ⎬ 2730
l : *los de Mahli* ⎫ *Merari*
m : *los de Mussi* ⎬ 3200
n : *Patio del Tabernaculo*
o : *Tabernaculo*
p : *Fuente de Miriam*
q : *Passo para el Tabernaculo*
r : *Riberas con sus lagos*
Escala

500   2000   4000

preserved attestation of the concept of the "Jerusalem above" is found in Paul's epistle to the Galatians. The idea is, however, of earlier origin, as it occurs both in Jewish apocalyptic and rabbinical writings.' 'This building now built in your midst is not that prepared beforehand here from the time when I took counsel to make Paradise' is a statement which illustrates the fusion of Jewish and Platonic traditions. After the fall of Jerusalem 'the brilliance of her glory and her majestic beauty' will appear visible on earth, a passage akin to the statement in Revelation mentioned above.[18] Furthermore, Philo's emphasis on the skill and memory of the architect, which is treated as a divine symbol in *De Opificio Mundi*, pays an indirect tribute to artistic creation, since the importance of planning the whole in conjunction with its parts is emphasized here.[19]

The process of adaptation, which led from a representation of the earthly Jerusalem to the medieval rendering of the

Engraving from Templo, showing the Tabernacle and the Israelites' tents. [See p. 26.]

Galatians IV, 26

2 Baruch IV, 3

4 Ezra X, 49–50
Revelation XXI

De Opificio Mundi, IV, 17–19 and V, 20

Sixth-century mosaic map (detail) in the Church of Madaba.

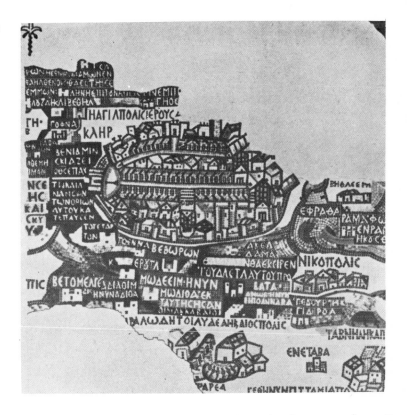

Heavenly City as a symbol, was slow. An interpretation of Jerusalem appears on a fragment of gilt glass from San Pietro e Marcellino, now in the Vatican Museum. This shows the Temple in the setting of a colonnade, surrounded by palm trees and houses. It is interesting to note that this religious conception is treated in a realistic manner, typical of Hellenistic art. In the 6th-century map in the church of Madaba, which is still realistic, Jerusalem forms a focal point. The perspective, a sort of oblique bird's-eye view, allowed the interior as well as the external walls to be shown.[20]

The Heavenly City is counterbalanced by the sinful town. This contrast between good and evil is expressly stated in the fourth Book of Ezra, with regard to Zion and Babylon. Babylon was characterized by snakes or dragons as, for instance, in *The History of the Destruction of Bel and the Dragon*. The theme of evil acting as the foil for the ideal proved a stimulant to the visual arts. Pictorially, the contrast is represented in the Synagogue of Dura-Europos, where the Jewish Temple and the temple of the sun-god are placed so that they express religious and moral opposites.

A far more ancient tradition existed in the numerous representations of walled townships as the background for battles in the ancient Orient. This tradition still persists in the

description of the Shield of Achilles in the *Iliad*, but with the   *Iliad*, Book XVIII
difference that scenes of marriage and submission to justice, and
of strife and treachery are contrasted in two cities. This may
perhaps be regarded as a 'moralization' of the theme, and the
question arises whether a sculptural prototype was used, or
whether this was a new literary convention.[21]

At any rate, it was the Jewish attitude which gave to the
architectural image the strength of a universal moral symbol,
a concept partly due, no doubt, to the Old Testament prohibition of pictorial renderings of living creatures. During late
Hellenism and the Roman period this prohibition was largely
ignored, especially in the historical cycles of the Synagogue of
Dura-Europos, but it retained some importance even there, as
is quite obvious from the emphasis placed on the contrasting
paintings of the Jewish Temple and the temple of the sun-god.[22]

The symbolic meaning attributed to cities persisted in
Christian art: Sodom and Gomorrah, the evil cities, are seen in
perspective in the Ashburnham Pentateuch of the 7th century,
a manuscript indebted to Jewish prototypes. Either Bethlehem
or Rome is coupled with Jerusalem on the triumphal arches of
basilicas in Rome and Ravenna.[23] The contrast between good
and evil cities, epitomized by Jerusalem and Babylon, persisted
as an iconographic theme throughout the Middle Ages. But in
the early Christian period the expression of redemption was
prevalent, and the preoccupation with the problem of sin seems
temporarily to have receded from artistic consciousness.

To sum up: during the Greek evolution the ideal plan was
isolated from its cosmological background; in a similar way
the magical connotations, although still felt, receded into the
background during Roman developments: Judaism contributed
the projection into the hereafter, and thus stressed the symbolic
aspects of the Messianic hope, as realized in the Heavenly
Jerusalem. The Greek, Roman and Jewish heritages influenced
the Middle Ages in the representation of ideal cities, either from
a formal point of view, or in a symbolic manner. How these
elements were fused and made their impact on the future will
be the theme of subsequent chapters.

1. *The Art and Architecture of the Ancient Orient*, Pelican *History of Art*, 1954, p. 55.
2. D. Nielsen, *Der Dreieinige Gott*, I, Copenhagen 1922, p. 302.
3. E. Unger, Babylon, *Die heilige Stadt*, etc., Berlin and Leipzig 1931. A. H.
   Layard, *The Monuments of Nineveh*, London 1849, pl. 30.
4. S. H. Hooke, *Myth and Ritual*, Oxford University Press 1933, *passim*; Lavedan
   I, *passim*; K. Lehmann, *The Dome of Heaven*, Art Bulletin 1945, p. 1 ff.; B. B.
   Smith, *Architectural Symbolism of Imperial Rome and the Middle Ages*, Princeton
   University Press, 1956.

5. cf. the important article in Pauly-Wissowa, 'Städtebau', by Professor Lehmann-Hartleben. Also *Dizionario Enciclopedico di Architettura e Urbanistica*, Rome 1968–9, under *Urbanistica* and *Mantinea*.

6. A convenient survey of Greek town planning, published in English, is found in R. E. Wycherley, *How the Greeks Built Cities*, London 1949. This work is largely based on the studies of A. von Gerkan, *Griechische Städteanlagen*, Berlin 1924.

7. E. Ivanka, *Die Aristotelische Politik und die Städtegründungen Alexanders des Grossen*, Budapest 1938. A short account of this theory is found in the article by S. Lang in *Architectural Review*, August 1952, p. 91 ff.

8. W. H. Roscher, *Ausführliches Lexikon der Griechischen und Römischen Mythologie*, Leipzig 1884, article 'Tyche'. M. Collignon, *Manual of Mythology*, translated by J. E. Harrison, London 1890, p. 303 ff.

9. H. Hunger, *Lexikon der Griechischen und Römischen Mythologie*, Vienna 1953, *passim*. The searching study of H. Gross, *Zur Entstehungsgeschichte der Tabula Peutingeriana*, Bremen 1913, is still worth reading, although the present writer disagrees with it on minor points of dating and interpretation.

10. Ch. Daremberg and E. Saglio, *Dictionnaire des Antiquités Grecques et Romaines*, article *Venti*. C. Thulin, *Religionsgeschichtliche Versuche*, III, 1906, especially the part on *Die Götter des Martianus Capella*, p. 1 ff. Also H. Rosenau in the *Journal of the R.I.B.A.*, October 1955, p. 481 ff. Divination by use of the liver had already been customary in Babylonia. M. Pallotino, *The Etruscans*, London 1955, p. 22 ff.

11. C. P. S. Menon, *Early Astronomy and Cosmology*, London 1932.

12. M. I. Rostovtzeff, *The Social and Economic History of the Roman Empire*, Oxford 1926 (new ed. 1958), and *The Social and Economic History of the Hellenistic World*, Oxford 1941. L. Friedländer, *Roman Life and Manners*, numerous editions, *passim*.

13. H. Jordan, *Forma Urbis Romae*, Berolini 1874. A new edition of this important monument is being prepared in Rome at the present time. cf. also Ch. Huelsen and H. Kiepert, *Forma Urbis Romae Antiquae*, Berolini 1912, and the relevant article in the *Enciclopedia Italiana* by G. Giovanoni.

14. H. Rosenau in *Palestine Exploration Fund Quarterly Statement* (1936), p. 157 ff., and also *A Short History of Jewish Art*, London 1948, *passim*, Part I, chap. 1. F. J. Hollis, *The Archaeology of Herod's Temple*, London 1934. The Biblical descriptions are largely based on the Second Temple. See also C. H. Krinsky, *Journal of the Warburg and Courtauld Institutes*, XXIII, 1970, p. 1 ff.; and A. Muehsam, *Coin and Temple*, Leeds University Press, 1966.

15. C. Roth, *Journal of Warburg and Courtauld Institutes*, XVI, 1953, p. 37. cf. the author's article in *The Journal of Jewish Studies*, 1972.

16. It is interesting in this connection that the ancient holy stone, the Ka'ba, is a cube. On its representation, cf. R. Ettinghausen in *Zeitschrift der Deutschen Morgenländischen Gesellschaft*, N.F. XII, 1934, p. 111 ff.

17. Menon, op. cit.

18. H. Rosenau, 'Contributions to Jewish Iconography' in *Bulletin of the John Rylands Library*, 1956, p. 475 ff. R. Wischnitzer, *The Messianic Theme in the Paintings of the Dura Synagogue*, Chicago 1948.

19. Translated by F. H. Colson and G. H. Whitaker for the Loeb Classical Library.

20. M. Avi Yonah, *The Madaba Mosaic Map*, Jerusalem 1954.

21. Pauly-Wissowa, articles 'Achilleus' and 'Schild'.

22. H. Rosenau, 'Contributions', op. cit. The latest work on the subject is edited by C. H. Kraeling, *The Excavations of Dura-Europos*, VIII, I, 'The Synagogue', Yale University Press, 1957. R. Wischnitzer in *Journal of the American Oriental Society*, 91, 1971, p. 367 ff.

23. cf. O. Demus, *The Mosaics of Norman Sicily*, London 1949, especially with regard to his references on iconography and chronology.

II

The Middle Ages

The survival of architectural traditions during the early Middle Ages is clearly illustrated in the legend connected with, or based on, the founding of the basilica of Santa Maria Maggiore in Rome. Pope Liberius was traditionally said to have drawn the ground-plan of the church after a miraculous fall of snow on the night of 4 and 5 August in the year A.D. 352. Among other examples of such miracles, the *Fundatio Ecclesiae Hildensemensis* refers to frost as providing the outline of the building, and a similar legend attaches to the Fraumünster in Zurich.[1] Furthermore, the founding and building of Santa Maria Maggiore is the theme of paintings by Sassetta, Masolino and Grünewald, and of a relief by Mino da Fiesole.

These traditions imply a continued awareness of planning, in spite of a loss of technical skill, combined with the prevailing belief that the execution of plans required more than human ability. In the monastic centres of early medieval learning and culture, the classical tradition persisted, and, as monasteries slowly took the place of cities, it is there that the earliest preserved designs were found, among them the Vitruvian diagram of winds of about A.D. 700.

This is one of the few existing examples of the illustrations for Vitruvius's treatise on architecture which pre-dates the Renaissance, although the work was originally clearly intended to include drawings. The main lines as well as the compass points are emphasized, whilst architectural detail is entirely omitted. The drawing therefore testifies to the continuation of the literary tradition, rather than to the transmission of technical skill. It was presumably executed in Jarrow and shows affinities with the *Codex Amiatinus*,[2] thus illustrating the widespread ramifications of Vitruvian influence.

The most outstanding example of medieval planning is the master or ideal ground-plan in the monastery of St Gall. It is Carolingian, probably of 818, and gives a comprehensive survey not only of the church, but also of the buildings devoted to schooling, the care of the sick, husbandry, agriculture and craftsmanship. The dedication to the Abbot Gozbert, addressed as *dulcissime fili* by an anonymous religious superior, makes clear the high ecclesiastical status of the sender. That the plan of

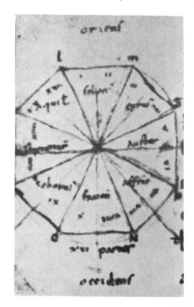

Vitruvius, Diagram of Winds. Harleian MS 2767, British Museum. (By courtesy of the British Museum)

32

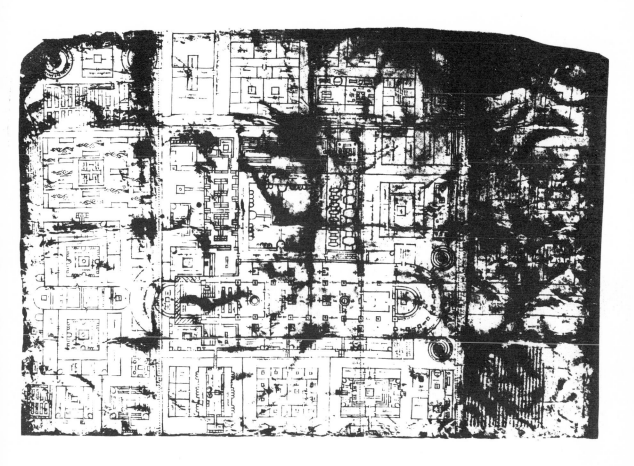

Ground-plan of the monastery, St Gall.
(By courtesy of the Monastery of St Gall)

St Gall was intended as a model is apparent not only from the comprehensiveness of the needs catered for, but also from the fact that measurements on a smaller scale were added to the church design at a later date, measurements which do not correspond to the building as outlined. Whether this was due to a change in the political and religious situation, the growing importance of the Aniane Reform (under Louis the Pious after the death of Charlemagne), or simply to the need for cheaper and less ambitious planning, one fact emerges clearly: the second church project was a much less important and smaller one, thus corroborating the ideal character of the earlier plan.[3]

The comprehensiveness of the original design, which has not been followed *in toto* either in St Gall or in any other known religious community, is further evidence that it was intended as a model from which guidance, rather than detailed instructions, could be derived. The basic rectangularity and regularity of the general layout is indebted to the classical heritage of Roman forts and camps, whilst the way in which a ground-plan is given follows the teachings of Vitruvius with regard to *ichnographia*. The plan of St Gall is thus the earliest extant

example of European planning surviving from the Middle
Ages, a document, originally no doubt one of many, which by
singular good fortune has escaped destruction.

Another example of medieval planning belongs to a basically
different type, since it is a record of the cathedral precincts and
grounds of Canterbury in the *Eadwin Psalter*, now in Trinity
College, Cambridge, probably drawn before or as a consequence
of the fire of 1174. This destroyed the Romanesque chancel,
seen on the design, which was replaced by the Gothic structure
of William of Sens. It may therefore have been executed under

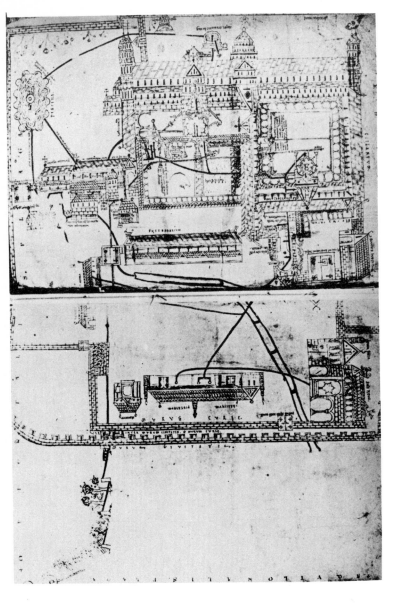

The precincts of Canterbury Cathedral;
from the *Eadwin Psalter*. (By courtesy of
Trinity College, Cambridge)

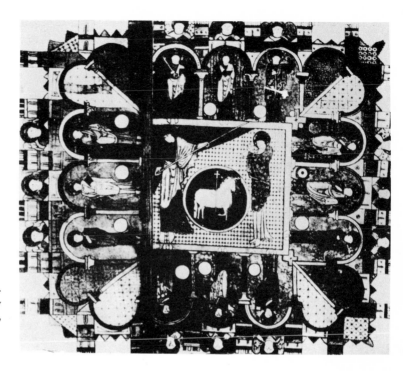

St John's vision of the Heavenly Jerusalem; from the *Beatus* of St Sever. (By courtesy of the Bibliothèque Nationale, Paris)
[See p. 36.]

the impact of the recent disaster, and may include improvements, especially as the drains or water pipes are carefully represented.[4]

The drawing may well have had a dual purpose: to show the improvements and also to describe and thus preserve the memory of the buildings as they existed before the fire, a theory corroborated by the handwriting, which, according to the late Dr R. E. W. Flower, can be dated about 1175.

The Canterbury drawing is not altogether an ideal plan, neither is it a working drawing, but a rare historical document, affording a survey aiming at exactitude and precision. It shows side views of the cloisters in combination with ground-plans, the whole united in an oblique bird's-eye perspective. Its technique as well as its purpose thus differentiate it from the ground-plan of St Gall. It is less near to classical prototypes, since the unsystematic mixture of different styles of representation is typically medieval, and far removed from the systematic teaching preserved in Vitruvius's writings. What is lost in abstract clarity is gained in a comprehensiveness which has a childlike quality, as when the fishpond and flowers are lovingly depicted without any desire for, or regard to, scale.

The examples mentioned above appear now as isolated instances, but must originally have been among numerous other drawings in which the classical heritage was adapted to the taste and requirements of the clergy. In this respect the most important theme during the Middle Ages seems to have been Jerusalem in its earthly and celestial aspects, since so many designs representing the subject have survived to this day. Jerusalem was identified with the Church by St Gregory the Great: '*Notandum est, quod non dicitur super quem erat aedificium, sed aedificium ut videlicet ostenderetur, quod non de corporalis, sed de spiritalis civitatis aedificio cuncta dicerentur . . . Et ipsa est civitas, scilicet sancta Ecclesia.*'[5]

The most telling example of the 'Heavenly Jerusalem', purged from realistic connotations, is perhaps found in the *Beatus* of St Sever in the Bibliothèque Nationale in Paris. This shows the figure of the Lamb, dominating the central square, flanked by the Angel with the rod and the figure of St John. The Apostles are seen within 12 separate gates, and the wall is surmounted by 12 angels. The city is ornamented by precious stones, symbolizing priceless value. As suggested previously, this square type of representation is based on the scriptural tradition.

The outline of the plan, reminiscent of medieval cloisters, the 12 gates and angels, the jewelled paving-stones, the angel with the measuring rod and the figure of St John, are all based on Revelation. The city coming down from Heaven is described. Walls and gates are seen as side views, the pavements as ground-plans, and the Lamb as a flat, heraldic design. Perspective appears to have been almost entirely omitted. The date of the MS belongs to the period of the rule of the Abbot Gregory, between 1028 and 1072. According to Neuss,[6] the *Beatus* MSS follow an ancient prototype of the 5th or 6th century; but this illumination is remarkable in that it shows a balance between formal interpretation and an elimination of perspective which was characteristic of the developed Romanesque style. It should therefore be regarded as a fairly independent composition, which did not accurately copy a model.

An interesting deviation from the typical arrangement is found in the *Scivias* of the great visionary, Hildegard of Bingen (1098–1179). The City of God is seen in the shape of a parallelogram, sited on a mountain, and set in a circle. The figure of Christ is seated at the apex, *Lucidus sedens*, and the winged head of the North Wind, *zelus dei*, protrudes from the left angle. This unusual and elaborately powerful image is based on a dynamic religious tradition, visually interpreted here with Christ appearing, quite literally, as the corner-stone of the building.[7]

An older style occurs in the illumination of the 'Heavenly Jerusalem' in the *Liber Floridus Lamberti* of Ghent, where numerous pictures of cities are found. The date is about 1120, and the work represents a typical example of the fusion of varying types of perspective, characteristic of the Romanesque.[8]

Babylon; from a *Beatus* MS. (By courtesy of the John Rylands Library, Manchester) [See p. 38.]

Here the Holy City, symbolizing the Church, is seen, but behind the abstract formal circular pattern the traditional perspective view of late Antiquity lingers on. The circle implies completeness and perfection, based on the Classical tradition. (*See* Frontispiece.)

The *corona*, the crown of light, is symbolized in the huge chandeliers hung, for example, in the third Abbey Church of Cluny, in the Cathedral of Bayeux, the Church of St Rémy in Reims, and in the cathedrals of Aachen and Hildesheim in

Eighteenth-century wall painting from the Synagogue of Mohilev, since destroyed, representing Worms as an evil city. From *Philolexikon* 1934.

Germany.[9] These fine works of craftsmanship show the city walls and the gates and towers of the Heavenly Jerusalem according to Revelation, although the numbers of these vary, and the square has been replaced by a circle. The meaning of these candelabra is pithily expressed in the words of Honorius Augustodunensis in *Gemma Animae*, discussing '*De Corona*':

Gemma Animae, I, 102

'Corona ob tres causas in templo suspenditur: una quod ecclesia per hoc decoratur . . . alia quod ejus visione admonemur quia hi coronae vitae et lumen gaudii percipiunt . . . tertia ut coelestis Hierusalem ,nobis ad memoriam revocetur.'[10]

Jerusalem; from a 12th-century *Passionale*. Landesbibliothek, Stuttgart.

The Palace of the Grail, the circular luminous abode described by the Younger Titurel in the 13th century, was equally influenced by the concept of the Heavenly Jerusalem. Its ground-plan was believed to have been miraculously traced on an onyx slab one morning, a legend reminiscent of those already mentioned.[11] By contrast, Babylon, surrounded by snakes, the symbol of evil, was found in numerous *Beatus* manuscripts, among them the one in the John Rylands Library, Manchester. This type of symbolic representation persisted and is still seen for example in the 18th-century painting of the Synagogue in Mohilev, now destroyed. Here the town of Worms takes the place of Babylon,[12] and the arrow-shaped tongue represents the evil nature of the 'worm'.

The most powerful artistic realization of the contrast between evil and redemption is not found in architectural images,

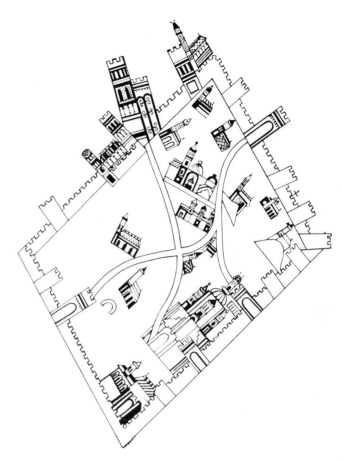

Jerusalem; after a 12th-century plan in
the Library at Cambrai.

however, but in the vision, crystallized by Dante in his *Divina
Commedia*: here, following Moslem prototypes, the funnel of
Hell is described; Jerusalem forms the centre of the known
globe and the Earthly Paradise is situated on top of the mountain of Purgatory, counterbalancing the vision of Hell, while
the heavenly spheres lead to the Empyrean.[13]

During the Middle Ages the celestial city seems to come
down to earth quite literally, because the abstract images are
slowly replaced by more realistic interpretations. Especially as
a result of the Crusades, interest in the Holy Land grew, and
the descriptions of pilgrims and the knowledge of eye-witnesses
made their impact. This is demonstrated, for example, by a
plan of the end of the 12th century, added to a *Passionale*, now
in the Stuttgart Landesbibliothek. Here is no longer the
Heavenly, but the earthly city, in which, contrary to scriptural
tradition, the inner part is surrounded by a circle of walls, a
form borrowed from coins. The names of churches, the tower
of David and the main roads, have been inscribed in Latin.
Accuracy was even further stressed in the plan in the Library
of Cambrai, where a rectangle limits the shape of the inner

town, which, as Père Vincent suggested, gives a comprehensive picture of the actual layout. It dates from about the same time, the transitional period between the Romanesque and Gothic styles.[14]

From these and other examples it would appear that medieval naturalism was more detailed and specific in intention than similar trends in the Hellenistic and Roman traditions, in which a general realistic impression rather than a particular interpretation was the aim. This interest in the specific, within a formalized art form, can also be seen clearly in the elaborate captions, which are so frequently included in medieval paintings. The process towards naturalism, starting in the late Romanesque and early Gothic periods, developed more and more strongly in the later phases of the Middle Ages, thus preparing the ground for the reception of the Italian Renaissance in the North.[15] Next in popularity to Jerusalem, although more realistically treated, was the depiction of Rome.[16] A link can be traced here from the antique heritage, through the Middle Ages, and up to the Renaissance, a link which is apparent in the retention of formal patterns and the vivid interest in the Eternal City. The most salient buildings, such as the Colosseum, are represented on Roman coins in isolation, but during the Middle Ages, the Colosseum, the Castle of San Angelo and many other buildings are shown in juxtaposition, while in the *Très Riches Heures* of the Duc de Berry of 1412–16, the city as a whole is seen in a traditional roundel, with a wealth of realistic detail and easily recognizable buildings.

Ambrogio Lorenzetti, Townscape of Good Government. Palazzo Pubblico, Siena. (Photograph: Anderson)

Slowly interest in the human element replaces the emphasis on architectural vision, and the ideal city appears filled with life. This transition gathered momentum in the Gothic period, when the towns became ever more significant social units and the Church ceased to be the sole, or an outstandingly prominent, patron of the arts.

In this development, the most important work is perhaps the cycle in the Sala dei Nove of the Palazzo Pubblico in Siena by Ambrogio Lorenzetti; this is not only a decorative masterpiece, but a sociological document of prime importance, dating from 1337–39. The two allegorical paintings show symbolic figures of Good and Bad Government; the former is also represented in a landscape depicting the blessings of tilled agricultural land in a realistic manner, and a view of urban life, shown against the background of the city's walls and houses. This urban life appears to be an aristocratic one, as the emphasis is on festive maidens and riders on horseback.

Unfortunately, the painting of the township representing Bad Government is in poor condition, but it still reveals that the architectural motifs are simpler; the buildings appear to be

Ambrogio Lorenzetti, Landscape of Good Government. Palazzo Pubblico, Siena. (Photograph: Anderson)
[See p. 40.]

Ambrogio Lorenzetti, Townscape of Bad Government. Palazzo Pubblico, Siena. (Photograph: Anderson)

in ruins and the inhabitants are fleeing or leaving, whilst soldiers make their way into the deserted city. A stylistically similar townscape, probably earlier and also presumably the work of Ambrogio Lorenzetti, evokes a sense of growth. Its slender towers, overlooking the open sea, are surrounded by walls.[17]

What is the relationship between ideal cities and the townships as they developed or were founded during the Middle Ages? The drawings of Villard de Honnecourt of the same period, and the plans for the enlargement of Siena Cathedral,

City by the Sea, probably by Ambrogio Lorenzetti. Siena Pinacoteca.

illustrate the techniques employed[18] and support the theory that on the whole it was the individual unit rather than the whole city which was planned. No designs for actual town-planning have survived, but the *bastides*, the 'New Towns' of the 13th century, clearly show that they were consciously and consistently conceived. They consisted of parallel streets; between these, the market square, the main church and fortifications stood out. In newly built towns, the towers fortifying the walls are usually similar in shape, not only for defensive reasons, but also because the Gothic style stressed regularity and uniformity, rather than variation and individualism. This principle can be studied particularly well in the planned towns in France and England. The clear division of co-ordinated streets, the *insulae* in the Vitruvian sense which provided the building plots, and the regular market squares with their adjoining churches and town halls, give a sense of enclosure and harmony. This may be experienced perhaps in its most satisfying form in Aigues-Mortes, started in 1241 by St Louis with the isolated main tower, and continued by Philip the Bold.[19] Here – because it failed to develop and expand – is a perfect medieval city, perfect for a limited period and a

Aerial view of Rouen, showing the impact of orientation. (Photograph Cie. Aérienne Française)

[See p. 44.]

particular site, but becoming quickly out of date. By contrast, because of their remoteness from life, the visions of ideal cities achieve a symbolic expression of timeless continuity and cannot be regarded as obsolete in the same sense.

Florence, as a prototype of the Italian medieval town, gains its very perfection from a different principle from that of royal patronage which operated in Aigues-Mortes: the conscious aesthetic efforts of its leading citizens. It is thus a monument to centuries of civic pride and endeavour, when continuity at a high level of individual taste was achieved. The citizens dispensed with overall planning and relied on communal co-operation within the given style.[20] This, broadly speaking, is characteristic of the main stream of evolution during the Middle Ages.

Perhaps the most important single factor which ensured regularity and homogeneity for the medieval township was the liturgical orientation of churches; this was maintained with few exceptions and gave an appearance of unified design to what is frequently now regarded as a picturesque site. This is particularly apparent in aerial views of medieval cities, among which Rouen is outstanding. The Cathedral of Siena is unusual, because here an attempt was made to change the traditional orientation by using the existing building as a transept and planning a new structure for the body of the church on a north–south axis.[21]

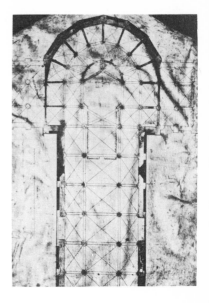

Medieval ground-plan of Siena Cathedral, describing the change of orientation. (By courtesy of Opera del Duomo)

Open, spacious market squares slowly developed during the 14th and 15th centuries, and vied with the religious precincts. Focal points, churches and town halls were emphasized, and they appear monumental, especially when compared to the smaller adjacent buildings which serve as a contrast and foil.[22] This is true even of the German medieval cities, such as Rothenburg, with its winding streets. In all cases, the protecting walls gave a sense of cohesion and enclosure; this they continued to do when *faux-bourgs* and suburbs came to be added to the older walled medieval towns. (It was in England alone that the peaceful open city flourished at an early period.) Thus a kinship existed between large castles and towns, a kinship emphasized by fortifications and the variety of trades and occupations required during a period of siege.[23] The artistic effect was achieved by identical or at least similar elements, bound to each other in a simple progression.

The medieval methods were successful so long as the towns remained small, and the addition of independent units had not yet led to unrestricted sprawl. However, the danger of the over-extended street already existed during the Middle Ages, especially in England, whilst Continental fortifications strengthened the habit of enclosure. Medieval reality was unrelated to the image of the ideal city, as represented by Jerusalem, whether heavenly or earthly, since here it was a unity of vision, and not the individual building or site, which dominated the effect.

Contemporary taste is clearly reflected in paintings. For example, in spite of the naturalism of the backgrounds, the foregrounds in the *Très Riches Heures* of the Duc de Berry in Chantilly appear independent and divided into parallel and regular strips. The pattern persists to the end of the Gothic period, and is still found in the basic environmental structure of the Madonna of the Chancellor Rolin by Jan van Eyck, for example.

The views expressed above are corroborated by a study of late medieval manuscripts, such as Jean Fouquet's illuminations

Jean Fouquet, The Entry of Ptolemy into Jerusalem; from *Antiquités Judaïques*. (By courtesy of the Bibliothèque Nationale, Paris)

to Josephus's *Antiquités Judaïques*, which show Jerusalem as a French contemporary town, with dominating individual buildings and regular streets. A similarly realistic interpretation is seen even earlier in the works of the van Eycks and their followers.[24]

Looking back over the ground covered, two main trends appear, which, though apparently contradictory, supplement and enhance each other. One is the slow transformation of the antique heritage in the direction of formal abstraction and elimination of detail, in order to emphasize the essential. The other is the growth of interest in describing the medieval city, with stress on realism and on the varied activities of the inhabitants. It is the latter trend which gains in historical significance and introduces the period commonly known as the Renaissance.

---

1. H. Rosenau, *Design and Medieval Architecture*, London 1934, *passim*.

2. Ch. Singer, *A History of Technology*, Oxford 1956, II, p. 527 ff. F. Granger, *Vitruvius on Architecture*, Loeb Classical Library, 1931–4.

3. J. Gantner, *Kunstgeschichte der Schweiz*, Frauenfeld and Leipzig 1936, p. 34 ff. W. Effman, *Die Baugeschichte des Hildesheimer Domes*, Hildesheim and Leipzig 1933, and *Centula*, Münster 1912. Also R. G. Collingwood with reference to Hyginus's *De Munitionbus Castrorum* in *The Archaeology of Roman Britain*, London 1930. Especially important is W. Böckelmann in *Zeitschrift für Schweizerische Archäologie und Kunstgeschichte*, XVI, 1956, p. 125 ff., with full bibliography, on the combination of two plans. For a survey in English, A. K. Porter, *Medieval Architecture*, Yale University Press, 1909, p. 147 ff.

4. R. Willis, *The Architectural History of the Conventual Buildings of the Monastery of Christ Church in Canterbury*, London 1869, is a detailed study, still worth referring to, especially p. 158 ff. cf. also the present writer in *The Burlington Magazine*, 1935, p. 128 ff.

5. H. Liebeschütz, *Das Allegorische Weltbild der Heiligen Hildegard von Bingen*, Hamburg 1930. Ch. Singer in *Studies in the History and Method of Science*, Oxford 1917 (and 2nd ed., London 1955), p. 1 ff. H. L. Keller, *Mittelrheinische Buchmalereien in Handschriften aus dem Kreise der Hiltgart von Bingen*, Stuttgart 1933. Dom. L. Baillet in Foundation Piot, *Monuments et mémoires*, 1911, p. 49 ff.

6. W. Neuss, *Die Apokalypse des Heiligen Johannes in der altspanischen und altchristlichen Bibelillustration*, Münster 1931, *passim*. For English examples, cf. P. Brieger, *English Art*, Oxford 1957.

7. cf. Liebeschütz, op. cit., also Ch. Singer, *From Magic to Science*, London 1928, p. 199 ff.

8. A. Böckler, *Abendländische Miniaturen*, Leipzig 1930, *passim*.

9. Of the older authorities, J. Sauer, *Symbolik des Kirchengebäudes*, Freiburg 1902, is still not superseded. A good illustration of the chandelier in the Cathedral of Hildesheim after restoration is found in *Das Münster*, X, 1957, p. 458. A fragment is reproduced in H. Picton, *Early German Art*, London 1939, pl. XCIV, 3. L. Kitschelt, *Die Frühchristliche Basilika als Abbild des Himmlischen Jerusalem*, Munich 1938, *passim*. This suggestive book takes far too literal a view of the correspondence between actual buildings and the symbolism of the Holy City, following H. Sedlmayr in *Die Entstehung der Kathedrale*, Zurich 1950. What is found during the Middle Ages is interpretation, not repetition; symbolism, not copying. A. Kitt's unpublished thesis, Vienna 1944, is un-

fortunately not accessible in this country.

F. Saxl, *A Memorial Volume*, ed. D. J. Gordon, Edinburgh 1957, contains an article by W. Oakeshott referring to *Mappae Mundi*, p. 245 ff. It has to be borne in mind that the *Mappa Mundi* may be regarded as an ideal plan, in so far as it reflects the activity of the Creator, and it is only in minor details that realism finds an unobtrusive field.

10. Sauer, op. cit., p. 182 ff. Migne, *Patrologia Latina*, CLXXII, 588 B.

11. L. I. Ringbom, *Graltempel und Paradies*, Stockholm 1951, stresses the Iranian influence on the grail motive, but neglects Revelation as a source. He rightly draws attention to the antagonism between Babylon and Rome. cf. also A. A. Barb in *Journal of the Warburg and Courtauld Institutes*, 1956, p. 40 ff., and the interesting article by A. Grabar in *Karolingische und Ottonische Kunst*, Wiesbaden 1957, p. 282 ff. It has to be borne in mind that some reliquaries are central buildings, reminiscent of the Dome of the Rock on the site of the Jewish Temple, which appears frequently in the 15th century as the characteristic building of Jerusalem, and, as it were, symbolizes the city. It is therefore of a different nature from that of the chandeliers, which, with their towers and gates, evoke the concept of the city as a whole.

12. M. R. James, *A Descriptive Catalogue of the Latin Manuscripts in the John Rylands Library at Manchester*, Manchester 1921, no. 8, p. 17 ff.

13. C. Vossler, *Medieval Culture*, London 1929. Rosenau, 'Contributions' op. cit.

14. A. Böckler, *Das Stuttgarter Passionale*, Augsburg 1923, pp. 6–7. Père L. H. Vincent, *Jérusalem nouvelle*, II, Paris 1922, p. 947 ff. Also M. de Vogüé, *Les Églises de la terre sainte*, Paris 1860, p. 407 ff., gives further designs; the one in Brussels is similar to the example from Zwiefalten.

15. F. Antal, *Florentine Painting and its Social Background*, London 1947, gives a fascinating account of this transformation.

16. M. Scherer, *The Marvels of Rome*, London 1956, *passim*.

17. O. H. Giglioli, *L'allegoria politica negli affreschi di Ambrogio Lorenzetti*, Emporium 1904, p. 265 ff. A detailed study of Ambrogio Lorenzetti is a desideratum; he is frequently underrated, as here, for instance by G. Sinibaldi in *I Lorenzetti*, Siena 1953. J. White, *The Birth and Rebirth of Pictorial Space*, London 1957.

18. On Villard, cf. H. R. Hahnloser, *Villard de Honnecourt*, Vienna 1935, *passim*. Particularly interesting is the sketch of a ground-plan of Vaucelles, pl. 28. On the significance of the cathedral, cf. also O. G. von Simson, *The Gothic Cathedral*, Pantheon Books, 1956, especially p. 11.

19. On Aigues-Mortes, cf. Lavedan I, p. 312 ff. A. Fliche, *Aigues-Mortes et St-Gilles*, Paris 1924, p. 8 ff. Also *Congrès Archéologique* (1950–1), p. 90 ff.

20. cf. W. Braunfels, *Mittelalterliche Stadtbaukunst in der Toskana*, Berlin 1953. This excellent study contains detailed documentation with regard to planning, especially for Florence and Siena. cf. also Antal, op. cit.

21. H. Rosenau, *Design*, op. cit., p. 22 ff.

22. Rosenau, *Design*, op. cit., p. 1 ff. T. F. Tout, *Medieval Town Planning*, first published in the *Bulletin of the John Rylands Library* in 1917, but still well worth reading. The notion of the picturesque as the dominating aesthetic factor in medieval town planning was introduced by C. Sitte in *Stadtbaukunst*, Vienna 1889. M. Beresford, *New Towns of the Middle Ages*, London 1967.

23. On castles cf. S. Toy, *Castles*, London 1939, *passim*. Also *A History of Fortification*, London 1955. Lavedan I, *passim*.

24. On illuminations, cf. P. Lavedan, *Représentation des villes*, Paris 1954. This book is a pleasant survey of pictures, but cannot be regarded as a serious historical study. The 'secret' of medieval masons is dealt with by P. Frankl and E. Panofsky in *Art Bulletin*, 1945, p. 46 ff.

III

The Early Renaissance

In town-planning the transition from the Middle Ages to the Renaissance was a slow and hesitant one. The main difference between the two periods is based on the contrast between the town with a small circumference, developed by gradually adding subsidiary parts – the *faubourgs* during the Middle Ages – and the Mannerist town, conceived as a centralized unit. Although the medieval representations of the cities of Jerusalem and Rome frequently showed a circular shape, this had little relevance to the realities of town-planning.

Building and planning took place against a changed social background during the Renaissance. The importance of the Italian cities, in turn conditioned by, and the outcome of, a growing secularization of life, led to an emphasis on formal values and the reinterpretation of the aesthetic tenets of the Ancients. The lavish culture depended on a wealthy class of merchant, which, during the Mannerist period, led to the establishment of the monarchy in Florence and to the incorporation of that city as the capital of the Dukedom of Tuscany.[1] The full programme of the Renaissance town was only rarely carried out; in most cases old cities such as Florence or Rome had to be adapted to the new taste, and although their beauty impressed future generations, the Renaissance planners presumably regarded them as haphazard creations.[2]

The marked difference between the Middle Ages and the Renaissance can best be clarified by the survival of so many artists' names in the latter period. True enough, the medieval artist did not always remain anonymous. Signatures and records have survived, but they are rare when compared with the self-expression in the writings of a Ghiberti or a Cennini, or the documentation found in the later writings of Cellini, Vasari or Condivi. It cannot be denied that a marked individuality, already noted by Burckhardt, characterized the Renaissance, an individuality based on the emergence of capitalism and a more secular society. Nevertheless, the Middle Ages were not entirely forgotten, and medieval reminiscences remained powerful and persistent.

It is in this context that Leone Battista Alberti (1404–72) and Antonio Averlino, who adopted the name of Filarete ('lover of virtue' – born *c.* 1400, died *c.* 1469), are placed. Alberti, famous as an architect and writer on diverse subjects – among them the blessings of family life, painting and architecture – made an outstanding contribution to the theory of town-planning in his *De Re Aedificatoria*. Filarete, a less well-known sculptor and architect, is a rather underrated author whose treatise, *Trattato d'Architettura*, deserves to be more widely known. Alberti, descended from the city aristocracy of Florence, was primarily a humanist. By contrast, Filarete had a practical involvement with his subject and seems to have been self-made; he had risen in status but still retained an awareness of the life of the common people, which gives his treatise a special charm and interest.

Unfortunately, as in the case of Vitruvius, no contemporary designs for the original edition of Alberti's treatise *De Re Aedificatoria* have been preserved, but the later editions and their illustrations form a valuable commentary on the changes of taste in different climates and periods. In fact a history of taste could be written with the help of such sequences of illustrations.

It is worth noting that the Alberti illustrations belong mainly to the 16th century, and are an important factor in establishing

Diagram of Winds; from the *Vitruvius Teutsch* of 1548.
[See p. 50.]

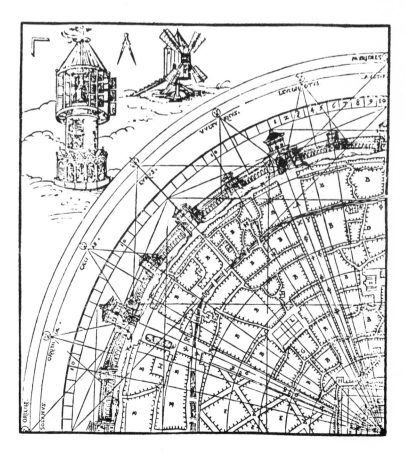

continuity; Jean Martin's posthumous French edition of 1553 is outstanding. The case of the Vitruvius editions is similar, with Fra Giocondo's illustrated one of 1511, Cesare Cesariano's of 1521, Martin's French edition (*Architecture ou art de bien bastir*) of 1547, and the compilation of the *Vitruvius Teutsch* by G. H. Rivius of 1548. Filarete, though his work was only printed in the 19th century and then only in part, was known from numerous manuscripts. Thus the thoughts of these three architects, Vitruvius, Alberti and Filarete, formed the background for future Renaissance developments.

Alberti deals with various aspects of the town: public buildings, premises for the principal citizens, the middle groups and the common people. The houses and villas of the rich are discussed, and soldiers' barracks, prisons and hospitals described. Although Alberti favoured round fortifications, he allowed variations dictated by the site. One must remember that the circular outline of city walls was already found in medieval paintings and coins, a preference reinforced by renewed Vitruvian and Platonic studies during the Renaissance.

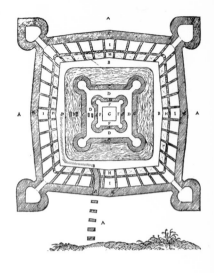

Alberti, Fortress of a Tyrant; from Martin's French edition.

Alberti, *De Re Aedificatoria*, IV, 5

What is original in Alberti is a frankly experimental attitude in his treatment of streets, which, he maintained, should be laid out 'in the manner of rivers', following an undulating pattern.[3] On the other hand, for large towns and fortified cities the approaches should be straight, to express greatness and dignity. He did not attempt the layout of a complete ideal town and advocated *commoditas* and the functional adaptation of sites to needs. He appreciated that the development of capitalism led to a more egalitarian rather than a stratified society; although the divisions according to social station were to be retained, and the more menial and smelly jobs located on the outskirts, he saw the advantages of having shopping facilities in the neighbourhood of aristocratic residences, thus achieving what is nowadays called 'a mixed development'.   VII, 1
Perhaps his most detailed contribution to planning is in the description of the tyrant's fortress city, which was to protect   V, 3
the palace equally against external and internal foes.

Alberti insisted that the city should possess a number of piazzas, without committing himself to a particular figure. He stressed moderation in size and decoration and deprecated ornamentation; the town should be neither too empty nor too small, and so avoid excess in either respect. The intimate relationship between the township and the private dwelling is emphasized, since the great house is regarded as 'a small city'.   I, 9 and V, 14

Although he continued medieval traditions, Alberti is mainly to be remembered as a precursor of modern, functional tastes, thus forming a link between the Middle Ages and the contemporary scene. His desire for naturalism in painting and his emphasis on simplicity and moderation, as well as his indebted-

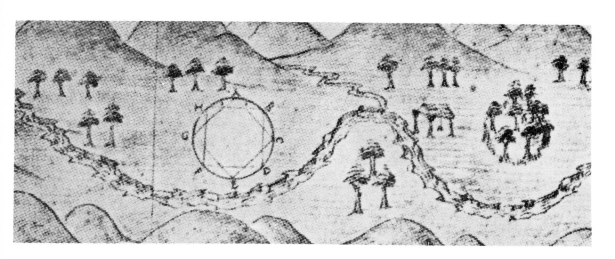

Filarete, Sforzinda in a Landscape; from the *Codex Magliabecchianus*. (By courtesy of the Biblioteca Nazionale, Florence)

ness to the Vitruvian tradition, are characteristic of his age. These few hints can obviously do no more than draw attention to the richness and versatility of Alberti's personality.

The first fully planned ideal city of the Renaissance was described and illustrated by Filarete about 1457–64. In his 'Treatise on architecture', of which the earliest fully illuminated

Filarete, ground-plan of Sforzinda. (By courtesy of the Biblioteca Nazionale, Florence)

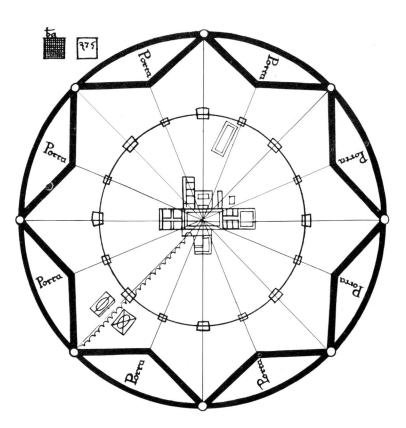

example preserved is the *Codex Magliabecchianus* in Florence, the fictitious city of Sforzinda and its surroundings are considered and the provision of building materials dealt with. The dedication was to Francesco Sforza, after whom the town was named. The Vitruvian Circle is indicated in the drawing, but the actual town was planned as an eight-point star made of two intersecting quadrangles, reminiscent of medieval tracery, and placed in a landscape; this was perhaps the earliest design combining town and country planning. (It is interesting to note that Filarete was also engaged in a treatise on agriculture, now unfortunately lost.) Filarete mentions that he made a model of the city for his patron. Gates were to be fitted in the inner angles and towers on the outer ones.

The concept of the creation of the ideal town as a task for man was a novel one, proclaiming civic pride and emphasizing human dignity, rather than religious preoccupation. Though churches are included, they leave pride of place to the palace, to austere and separate schools for boys and girls, to the prisons and the house of 'Vice and Virtue', which was intended to add

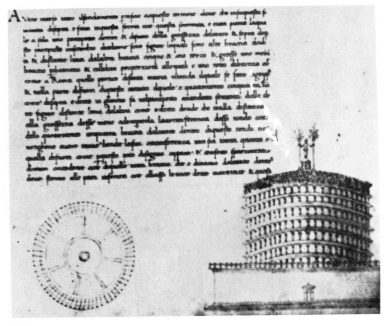

Filarete, House of Vice and Virtue. (By courtesy of the Biblioteca Nazionale, Florence)

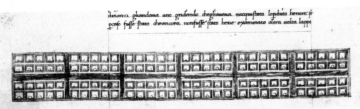

Filarete, Artisans' Dwellings. (By courtesy of the Biblioteca Nazionale, Florence)

Filarete, Hilly Landscape. (By courtesy of the Biblioteca Nazionale, Florence)

to the moral perfection of the citizens. The latter was truly comprehensive in conception, consisting of a ring of 10 storeys on a square base, erected on a socle, and crowned by the statue of Virtue. The structure was to contain lecture rooms, a brothel at the bottom, and an academy of learning in the higher storeys, culminating in provision for the study of astrology at the top.

Artisans' cottages and a small colony for workmen are included in the town of Sforzinda, as the aim is to cater for the needs of all classes. Filarete also designed a hospital for the town, similar to the one he built in Milan.[4] His interest in social problems is further indicated by a description of mountain dwellers in their great poverty. He comments on their gipsy-like appearance, their whitish, that is, undyed clothing, and their pale faces. Particularly significant is his interest in landscape, foreshadowing Leonardo da Vinci and Dürer; this is apparent not only in his description of the ironworks, but also in the introduction of canals to the town and to the artisans' quarters, providing them with easy access to water.

Sforzinda is distinguished by a fully developed town-centre with a main square. Sixteen subsidiary squares with alternative functions provide markets and open spaces for churches. Canals connect the main piazza and outlying districts in a manner reminiscent of Venice. The detailing is adapted from the Vitruvian alternation of winds and streets. Every second street is replaced by a waterway, and colonnades adorn the main squares and thoroughfares. Outside the town a 'labyrinth' was to surround the citadel, like that of 'Daedalus and the Minotaur'. Here Filarete gives rein to his imagination and is perhaps the first architectural writer to combine archaeological fancy with function.

The sixth book of Filarete's treatise deals with the citadel and the layout of the centre of Sforzinda, which is designed to include three squares, two of which are adjacent to the main piazza, to the north and south. The first includes the cathedral and the prince's palace, while the remaining two are allotted to the merchants and the market. They are surrounded by important buildings: the *podesta*'s palace, the bank and the mint, and the palace of the constable and the baths, respectively. This can perhaps be regarded as the first hint of what developed later as multifocal planning.[5]

It is likely that Francesco Colonna's *Hypnerotomachia of Poliphilo*, published in 1499,[6] presupposes acquaintance with Filarete's writings, which were far more influential than is generally conceded. For example, the framing story used by Boccaccio is given by Filarete as an excuse for discussing architectural ideas and his detailed interest in sculpture, not merely as a decorative factor, but as a telling means of expressing shows the function of the building concerned.

Indeed, Filarete's influence was still felt during the High Renaissance and the Mannerist period. Although his treatise remained unpublished until the last century, the manuscripts of his work, originally in Italian and also in Latin translation, were numerous and scattered all over Europe. His influence radiated widely, outside as well as inside Italy, and should be considered with that of Vitruvius and Alberti.

The illumination with Egyptian motifs of the *Missal of Pompeo Colonna*, now in the John Rylands Library, Manchester, dated presumably about 1520,[7] is particularly interesting, since it follows a pictorial tradition established by the obelisk carried on an elephant in the *Hypnerotomachia of Poliphilo*. It is remarkable that this complete survey of Egyptian forms gives a sort of catalogue of the known decorations. The desire for completeness, unusual at the time, foreshadows the archaeological interest of the 18th century, which led eventually to the functional adaptations of Egyptian forms, especially by Boullée and Ledoux.

Francesco di Giorgio Martini (1439–1502), a famous builder of fortifications, may be compared with Filarete in his interest in town-planning, but he differs in his emphasis on realistic achievements and his interest in geometric forms, which include various combinations of figures. The third book of his *Trattato di architettura*, presumably written late in life and completed in 1495, is devoted to castles and cities; the fifth to fortifications. He forms a link between the planners and formalists of the subsequent Mannerist phase of the Renaissance, especially in his design of a spiral city on a hilltop. The Mannerist planners in turn transmitted his work and the Vitruvian tradition to later generations.[8]

The High Renaissance

Famous and familiar names are numerous during the period of the High Renaissance, among them the great Italians – Leonardo, Michelangelo and Raphael. In Germany Dürer was at work, perhaps the greatest artist that country ever produced, and in England Sir Thomas More coined the term 'Utopia', for an imaginary country which incorporated many traits of contemporary England. None of these men were primarily or solely architects, but they were fascinated in varying degrees by the image of perfection in an ideal city. They can in this respect be regarded as exceptional rather than typical of their period, since a sense of personal achievement and contentment was more characteristic of the time: a preoccupation with the present, rather than an endeavour to command the future.[9]

In the work of Leonardo da Vinci (1452–1519), the individual building or the landscape as a whole with its geological and topographical features, rather than the isolated town, is the centre of interest. However, a city partly underground is seen in designs found in the Manuscript B of the Institut de France. These show two levels, one high, the other below it, and a network of straight streets, the upper ones for the gentry, those beneath for freight and services. The lower parts of the houses and the underground streets receive no direct light and are

Leonardo da Vinci, Project for a City partly Underground. Manuscript B, L'Institut de France.

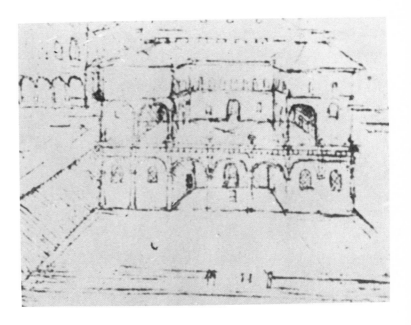

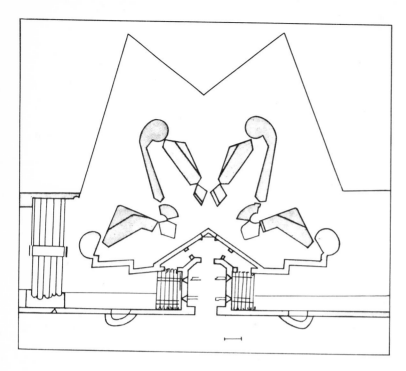

Study for Fortifications, after Michelangelo. Uffizi, Florence.

dependent on openings in the streets above. The use of the
lower rows of buildings – perhaps destined for the service staff
of the mansions above – is not explicitly mentioned in Leonardo's
notes. Considerable emphasis was placed on technical achievements, shown, for instance, in the drawings for movable and
adjustable – in fact, prefabricated – houses.

These examples illustrate some of the manifold interests,
as well as the inhuman detachment, of Leonardo, qualities
brilliantly analysed by S. Freud, but which set the artist apart
from the majority of town-planners, who, even if less gifted,
are primarily concerned with the human rather than the
technical element in planning.[10]

Michelangelo (1475–1564), who exerted a powerful influence
on the next generation of Mannerist planners, should be
mentioned in this context since, although not primarily
concerned with town-planning, he was responsible for part of
the fortifications of Florence in 1529, for which he developed
tooth and pincer-shaped bastions, far in advance of their time.
They express a spirit of attack rather than defence. He left
numerous unexecuted designs for this work, but unfortunately
few have survived. His fight against the Medici as well as for
Civita Vecchia and the Borgo in Rome, and his desire for civic
liberty, are of significance in the history of town-planning, and
his lasting influence in matters of fortification should not be
overlooked.[11]

Raphael (1483–1520), whose universal spirit and humane attitudes distinguish his paintings, was in charge of St Peter's and of other important buildings. Appointed 'Maestro delle Strade', he became the town-planner of the three great Roman arteries, the Corso and the two roads radially connected with it. As Conservator he was either the author of, or connected with, a plan of ancient Rome and a *Memoriale* on antiquities. This ideal Rome, which he projected into the past, foreshadowed the future of 17th-century developments. To quote verses attributed to Celio Calcagnini, the Apostolic Protonotary: *Romam in Roma querit reperitque Raphael.*[12]

Albrecht Dürer (1471–1528) was comparable in scope to the greatest Italian artists. In his searching spirit he showed affinity to Leonardo, but differed from him temperamentally in his sympathetic warmth and concern for human beings, their joys and sufferings. The extent of his studies included proportion and anatomy, as well as perspective, and in his later years he extended his interests to town-planning. He developed two kinds of fortification in his book, *Etliche Underricht zu Befestigung der Stett, Schloss und Flecken*, published in 1527. The more realistic, circular type of *Clause* continues an old tradition with its round keep, whilst the square outline of the fortress may not only be suggested by the Vitruvian Atrium or the Heavenly Jerusalem, but is in all probability based on such famous 14th-century Italian castles as the Castello d'Este in Mantua of about 1385, or the Castello di Corte in Ferrara of 1395–

Dürer, circular ground-plan of a Fortress; from *Etliche Underricht*.
[See p. 58.]

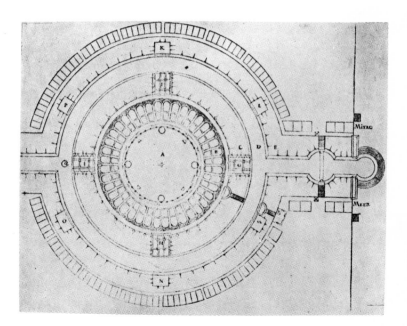

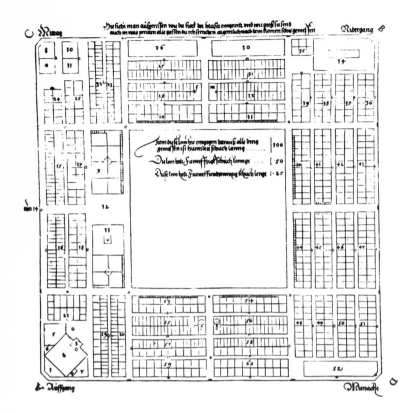

Dürer, square ground-plan of a Fortress;
from *Etliche Underricht*.

1406.[13] Similar in outline and plan is the representation of the
Castle of Milan in Rivius's *Vitruvius Teutsch* of 1548. Rivius,
unconcerned with the earlier history of the castle, attributes
the fortifications to a later date, the initiative of Francis I of
France. In Perrault's edition of Vitruvius the ancient plan is
elaborated to include a central forum.

As to the suggestion by Palm that Dürer may have been
influenced by the plan of Tenochtitlán, newly published in
1524, the opposite may well be true: Tenochtitlán was represented in woodcuts in the German tradition, therefore any
resemblance to Dürer's plans may be due to a similarity of style,
rather than to mutual influence.[14]

Dürer's quadrangular designs, belonging to the more extended and imaginative project, envisaged a complete town,
with a central castle in an open square, a church situated in a
corner, shops and workshops for artisans, granaries – in fact
all the necessities required during a long siege. In accordance
with Alberti's teaching, the house had become a small city.
Apart from formal considerations, the relegation of the church
to a corner reflects the change in religious emphasis brought
about by the rising tide of the Reformation.

In the development so far outlined, More's (1478–1535) architectural descriptions in *Utopia*[15] find a place, since his concern is social as well as formal. The chief town, Amaurot, is regular, almost a square, the wider side being near the river, the narrower on the hill – a significant English concession to the site. The other cities also show an almost geometric shape, as far as their location permits, and all are provided with identical rows of houses, making for regularity. 'He that knows one of their towns, knows them all . . . its figure is almost square, for from the one side of it, which shoots up almost to the top of the hill, it runs down in a descent for two miles to the river.' The integration of town and country seen here sets More apart from his predecessors, except Filarete, as does his concern for agriculture: 'That which is so universally understood among them, that no person, either man or woman, is ignorant of it.' His cities are not to contain more than 6,000 families, and surplus children are to be forcibly removed to ensure this.[16]

It is significant, however, that the woodcut accompanying the first edition of 1516 remains in the medieval tradition so far as architecture is concerned: the buildings are Gothic, and only the irregular outline of the island, which should be a crescent, shows a vague relationship to the text. This illustrates how far More's taste was not only in advance of his time, but also of his illustrator and publisher.

Below left
View of the Castle of Milan; from the *Vitruvius Teutsch* of 1548.

Below right
Sir Thomas More, Frontispiece from *Utopia*.

The Mannerist Phase

The appeal of the High Renaissance remained dominant, until, in the late 16th century, a slow change set in; this made for specialization, for social divisions into rigid conventional strata, and thus led to the aftermath of the Renaissance, commonly known as Mannerism. The reasons for such developments were the new centralized states; the ascendance of Spanish taste; the replacement of republics by hereditary monarchies, as in Florence; the threat of wars and invasion by external foes; the growing impact of, and reaction against, the Reformation as a political factor; and economic competition, especially between France and the Netherlands.[17]

A great deal of emphasis has hitherto been given to the architectural elevations of the Mannerist period, but comparatively little attention has been focused on the ground-plans in their finite regularity. In this period the town-planners' ideas were practically applied, or, if this proved impossible, they flourished at least on paper. Architects designed regular layouts of formal perfection, destined mainly for military purposes. Their fortresses and fortified towns were based on the traditions of Vitruvius and Filarete.[18] Renaissance and Mannerist architects were concerned with climate and landscape, but they did not yet see the problems of population size.

The programmatic expression of the tendencies of the Mannerist phase is found in the title of the treatise by Vincenzo Scamozzi (1552–1616), *L'Idea della Architettura Universale* (first published in 1615, and republished, translated and re-edited in many European languages throughout the 17th century), which

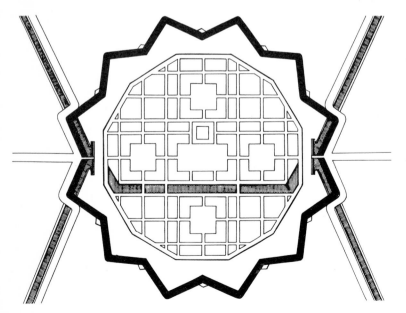

Scamozzi, ground-plan of an Ideal City; after *L'idea della architettura universale*.

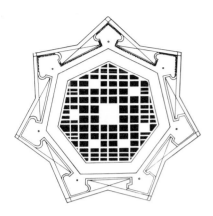

Cataneo, ground-plan of an Ideal City; from *L'architettura*.

Reproduced on p. 52 *r.* and *v.* of *Della Fortificatione*

Ground-plan of Palmanova, after an ancient engraving.

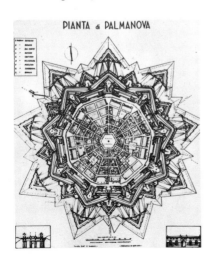

influenced such well-known popularizers' work as Fréart de Chambray's *Parallèle de l'architecture antique avec la moderne*, published in 1650. Scamozzi's comprehensive treatise, after giving a survey of Roman model buildings, lays down rules for planning the ideal city. It should be regularly divided into five open spaces, the purpose of each defined as suggested by Filarete, to whom Scamozzi refers in the index of his *Architettura*. The central, larger square was allocated to the town-hall, the *Signoria*, whilst the four subsidiaries were given over respectively to exchange and business; the general market; the sale of vegetables and fruit; and the sale of wine and livestock.

Another, smaller square counterbalances the river, which is of regular form, like a canal, and adds a touch of asymmetry as a special refinement within the symmetrical shape. An alternative design was mentioned by Scamozzi for a smaller city, which was to contain only three squares.

Brief mention should be made of Pietro Cataneo's publication *L'Architettura*, of which the first four books were published in Venice in 1554, and an enlarged version in 1567. Here geometrical patterns dominate and the treatise includes public buildings, sacred and profane. The aim is often formal balance, rather than absolute symmetry of detail.

The engineer and writer Girolamo Maggi and the captain and engineer of the King of France (presumably Henry III), Iacomo F. Castriotto, produced an original volume in their joint treatise: *Della Fortificatione delle Città*, published in Venice in 1564. They dealt here with fortifications, but also with the layout of the towns themselves, still showing Filarete's influence in the market square, but adding a dominating tower.

Palmanova, the fortress city of Venice begun in 1593, with its central tower in the market square, is indebted to Filarete's *Sforzinda* and is frequently attributed to Scamozzi, but may have been inspired by the second book of Maggi and Castriotto's publication. An early example of the realization of an overall-planned, homogeneous township, Palmanova was destined to remain in the backwater of future developments; it is now sleepy and provincial, reminiscent of a powerful tradition designed to regulate life in a rational pattern.

The emphasis during this period was on regularity and dignity, the rule of fitting conduct, and the importance of social restraint, coupled with a widespread feeling of disillusion and isolation. Perhaps it is partly for this last reason that Mannerism has a certain vogue at the present time.[19] The social element in the concept of the ideal city of the Renaissance was replaced by formalism, by a preponderance of the regular, geometric plan, paradoxically combined with a utilitarian approach, due to the pervading necessity of fortifications and fortified towns. The formalistic appeal of these designs is coupled with skill and

Serlio, the Tragic, Comic and Satyric
(p. 63) 'Scaenas', in the original Vitruvian sequence.

inventiveness in engineering, the practical and the aesthetic thus being combined in a contradictory manner, different from, and opposed to, the powerful integration found in the earlier phase of Renaissance planners. This dichotomy is perhaps the most characteristic feature of the later period.

But the influence of ideal planning went further: in the aristocratic society there were patrons who appreciated the subtle relationship between the stage play and its architectural background, the most famous example of which was Palladio's Teatro Olimpico in Vicenza. To the same type of fixed structures belonged Serlio's designs for comedy, tragedy and the satyr play, based on, but changing, the Vitruvian sequence; by using Gothic, Classical or 'rustic' forms, the fundamental meaning of the play concerned was illustrated. The theatre streets of Serlio (1475–1554) vividly express the change from the Renaissance; they are no longer models for realization in actual buildings, but patterns of make-believe, pleasing effects for their own, that is, art's sake. The basically optimistic attitude which believed in the creation of the ideal city – even if only in the hereafter or in a future almost as remote – was replaced by a disillusioned outlook allied to the formalism and rigidity of the emerging centralized state and its class divisions.

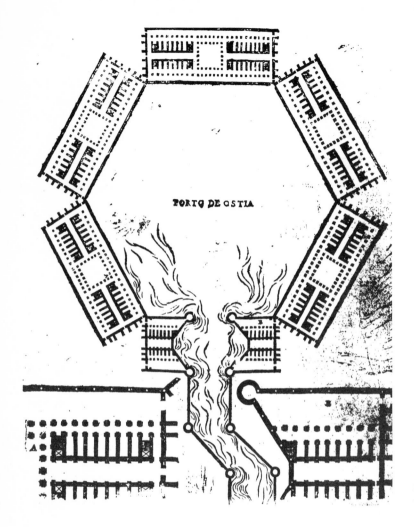

PORTO DE OSTIA

Serlio, reconstruction of the Harbour of
Ostia.

A landscape used as the background for the rustic is self-
explanatory, and primitivist in character (to use Boas's and
Lovejoy's term); Classical forms are confined to high tragedy,
and Gothic motives are reserved for the lower art of comedy,
which obviously requires less decorum.[20]

It seems an exaggeration to suggest on this and kindred
evidence that the theatre influenced the town-planner; the
reverse seems to have been the case. From Alberti and Filarete
onwards, the ideal city had occupied the minds of Renaissance
architects, and it was from here that the theatre designers
derived their inspiration. None the less, the theatre did undoubtedly influence book illustrations, such as those showing
fantastic structures in the *Hypnerotomachia of Poliphilo*.

In Serlio's writings and their illustrations are elaborate
instructions for perspective constructions, and among his studies
antique prototypes suggest formative patterns, as, for example,

in the detailed layout of Diocletian's Palace in Spalato, presented as a large square, or his hexagonal plan for Trajan's harbour in Ostia, based on the ancient ruins and Pliny's text of the *Historia Naturalis*.[21]

Serlio, who was appointed architect of Fontainebleau in 1541, exerted a powerful influence in France. Indeed, it appears that the rationalism of the Mannerist phase was so easily incorporated in the French tradition that the French succeeded in becoming, so to speak, more Italianate than the Italians. As a result Girolamo Cataneo's treatise, *Opera nuova di fortificare* (Brescia 1564), was translated into French and published in Lyon in 1574 under the title of *Le Capitaine*, whilst Jean Martin's work as a translator popularized Vitruvius and Alberti.

Martin's edition of *Vitruvius*, mentioned above, was dedicated to the 'Roy Treschrestien', Henry II of France; it was adorned with a complicated variety of woodcuts of high artistic quality, some executed by Jean Goujon, ranging from the erection of the primeval hut to the 'symmetry' of the human body. Serlio's views of the theatre are also included; they had previously appeared in the combined Italian and French edition of his first and second books on architecture, both of which had been translated by Martin in 1545. Goujon adapted freely from the Venice editions of Vitruvius, enlarging them, and adding new

Goujon, Primeval Huts; from Martin's *Vitruvius*.

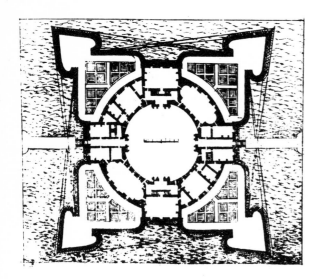

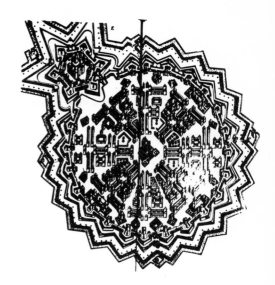

and formally evocative details. In his rendering of the primeval hut, Goujon was probably influenced by the Filarete illustrations, which include Adam's first building, although he has increased the number of posts of the basic structure. Filarete, in turn, had been influenced by Vitruvius's descriptions, and this illustrates the complicated manner in which the cross-currents of Mannerist artistic thought operated. Indeed, concern with the primitive hut, based on the Vitruvian tradition, persisted right into the 17th century, as one can see from Claude Perrault's French translation of Vitruvius of 1684.

The Renaissance tradition was continued in France by Iaques Androuet Du Cerceau (c. 1500–c. 1584), outstanding among the architect-engravers. In his *Livre d'architecture* of 1559, he published a number of comprehensive plans for large single buildings, mainly palaces; these were based on Italian theory in their respect for symmetry and their emphasis on the circle. In the 1615 edition of Du Cerceau's work are numerous fortified mansions, designed like comprehensive small town units, some of them perhaps the work of his son of the same name.

More pedestrian, and for this reason more easily realized, were the geometric designs for various fortified towns by Iaques Perret in *Des fortifications et artifices*, first published in Paris in 1601. The book includes centrally planned and varied layouts, and a citadel with central tower. He is still indebted to Filarete in the arrangement of the main piazza: '*ceste grand-ville a 23 costez*'. Perret adds the high tower to the piazza rather than the citadel, presumably influenced by the second book of *Della fortificatione* by Maggi and Castriotto, as well as the engravings of Palmanova. He differentiated between the *grand'rue* and

Above
Perret, an Ideal City; from *Des fortifications et artifices*.

Above left
A Fortified Mansion; from the posthumous edition (1615) of Du Cerceau's *Architecture*.

Perret, *Des fortifications*, plates D1 and 2
Des fortifications, plates E1 and 2

Des fortifications, plate K

Gargantua, LIII

Perret, a Skyscraper Palace.

petite rue and was interested in traffic problems, as well as in the relationship between the fortified castle and the town. Perret was concerned not only with cities, but with country houses and castles. These, unlike Palladian villas, had compact ground plans and Gothic touches in their decoration. He also designed *temples*, Huguenot churches, and a royal palace in the form of a skyscraper, perhaps to facilitate defence during the religious wars. His publication, simplified in layout and details, influenced the designs for the 'new towns' of Henrichemont, founded by Sully in 1608, and Charleville, the creation of Charles de Gonzague, begun in 1606.[22]

Perret's contemporary, Claude de Chastillon, planned a Place de France for Paris, in 1604, according to Bauchal. The scheme was engraved in 1610, and shows a development on Vitruvian lines: half a polygon abutting a canal.

In literature a reflection of the taste for regularity is found in Rabelais's description of the Abbey of Thélème in *Gargantua*, published in 1534, according to A. Lefranc. The abbey is a hexagon with large towers at the angles, and has six storeys containing 9,302 rooms.[23] Similarly, the French ceremonial *entrées* of the period, such as Henry II's *entrée* into Rouen, are indebted to the tradition of the Mannerist planners.[24]

Although in the drawings of towns, circular and polygonal plans generally predominated, in Germany Dürer's square outline had lasting influence. This can be seen in Freudenstadt, designed by the architect Heinrich Schickhardt (1558–1634), where the design of the open square with the church set in a corner is repeated. Through the intermediary of Schickhardt, Johann Valentin Andreae, the Protestant theologian, conceived of an ideal square in *Christianopolis*[25]; its parallel lines of regular houses are terraced and continuous in a rectangular layout, the latter feature being indebted to More's Utopia. And the German architect, Daniel Speckle or Speklin (1536–89), who interpreted the Italian prototypes in a distinct, if rather provincial manner, included in his towns large, empty, central piazzas, while expressing his national concern and adding an individual note in his treatment of rivers, the sea and hills. The formal, stylistic developments of Mannerist town-planning, and its emphasis on fortification, retained their influence throughout the Baroque period and up to the 18th century.[26]

In the so-called *Memoirs* of Gaudentio di Lucca, published in London in 1737 (thought to have been written by an Englishman, Simon Bevington), the Utopian tradition based on More still operates as far as the similarity of the towns, the emphasis on agriculture and other items are concerned. But di Lucca added a reinterpretation in the fashionable rococo style, with a central *place* or piazza surrounded by houses with concave façades; and he also advocated avenues lined by cedar trees.[27]

Continuity of the tradition is also illustrated by the prison of La Force in Ghent, and Bentham's 'Panopticon'.[28]

In conclusion, it may be useful to consider how far town-planning influenced painting.[29] The ideal image of the city and the transition from Renaissance to Mannerism certainly appears in the architectural backgrounds of contemporary Italian paintings, but in the North we find a portrait of the city as individual as the human face.

To give a few examples only: Piero della Francesca depicts individual structures in the frescoes of San Sepolcro in Arezzo; Perugino's 'Sposalizio' of about 1500 and his 'Handing of the Keys to St Peter' in the Vatican still reveal the isolation of simple, symmetrical buildings; and the same tendency is seen in the realistic Florentine streets in Ghirlandaio's paintings, where the individualism of the early Renaissance finds expression. Raphael's 'School of Athens', painted between 1508 and 1513, epitomizes the High Renaissance with its monumental and balanced architecture, within which human beings are neither dwarfed nor exalted, but contribute to a harmonious sense of unity.[30]

However, in the Mannerist period the emphasis is on types. In portraiture, reserve replaces alertness: *Diskretion statt Bereitschaft wird zur Vorschrift*, as Niels von Holst put it.[31] In architecture, the fortified town replaces the warrior's physical strength and represents the cleavage between formalism and utilitarian needs. A similar duality is apparent in El Greco's rendering of Toledo, now in the Museo del Greco.[32] He reveals a pronounced preoccupation with exactitude, since the view is supplemented by a ground-plan, but an elaborate inscription is added which is an apology for the lack of realism in the siting of the Hospital of Don Juan Tavera – so that it should not obstruct the view of the city gate – and for changing the direction of its façade. To enhance the element of unreality, however, the Hospital is seen resting on a cloud.

This brief survey attempts to clarify the way in which the Mannerist planners narrowed the social purposes of the preceding Renaissance, and how, working for the aristocracy, they developed a circumscribed and formalized type of architecture, in which the fortified township was dominated by geometric patterns.

The question then presents itself: to what extent are the Mannerist plans ideal, that is, perfect and visionary? Certainly they contain no socially or formally original or impossible provisions; indeed, they have been extensively used in such 'new towns' as Palmanova, Charleville, Henrichemont, Coeworden and others. These are all circular, polygonal or square, but, as they are meant to serve a practical purpose, the outer fortifications may not always follow the design of the inner town, and streets may break up the angles of the squares; furthermore, minor ornamental motifs and asymmetries detract from the formalism of the main design. Thus two main trends are apparent in the plans: the utilitarian aim and the emphasis on formal patterns, while individual and social considerations are neglected. Each of these trends had its own sphere of influence, and this meant that the Mannerist period was one of the most potent forces in the history of European architecture.

It has been seen how the early Renaissance freed the concept of town-planning from the medieval, chiefly religious and symbolic, interpretation. This was even further challenged during the High Renaissance, when the concept of the unity of the town tended to disappear; the emphasis was then on the individual contribution, based on clarity and accuracy of observation, and formal considerations of symmetry. In the Mannerist phase, the unity of the town was re-established by a more restricted, purely formal, approach, coupled with material – namely military – considerations, thus creating a dichotomy which led to easily applicable, but socially sterile, patterns.

---

1. On the problems cf. the writer's article in the *Festschrift Martin Wackernagel*, Cologne-Graz 1958, p. 185 ff. On the social background, cf. Antal's standard work, op. cit.

2. On the Renaissance generally and on unity and proportion in particular, cf. R. Wittkower, *Architectural Principles in the Age of Humanism*, London 1949 (1st ed.).

3. The best edition of Alberti's architectural treatise is still the German one by M. Theuer, published in Vienna and Leipzig in 1912.

4. The hospital of Milan, originally designed by Filarete, is now part of Milan University.

5. W. von Oettingen's edition, published in Vienna in 1890, is still valuable and has not been superseded by the work of M. Lazzaroni and A. Munoz, *Filarete*, Rome 1908. L. Firpo's *La città ideale del Filarete*, in *Studi in memoria di G. Solari*, Torino 1954, contains little that is new. According to von Oettingen the brothel was situated with the baths, a typical arrangement (p. 209). A facsimile edition of the work of Filarete has been published by J. R. Spencer: *Filarete's Treatise on Architecture*, Yale University Press, 1965. J. Onions in *The Journal of the Warburg and Courtauld Institutes*, XXXIV, 1971, p. 96 ff.

6. Among the numerous editions of Poliphilo, the one by C. Poplin, Paris 1883, is outstanding. It consists of the French translation, published in 1545, the woodcuts, and an interesting introduction.

7. M. R. James, *A Descriptive Catalogue of the Manuscripts in the John Rylands Library*, Manchester 1921, nos. 32–7, p. 87 ff.

8. A. S. Weller, *Francesco di Giorgio*, Chicago 1943.

9. On the Renaissance ideal, cf. H. Wölfflin, *Classic Art*, London 1952.

10. cf. J. P. R. Richter, and I. A. Richter, *The Literary Works of Leonardo da Vinci*, 2nd ed., Oxford University Press, 1939, II, especially nos. 741–2. S. Freud, *L. da Vinci*, New York 1916.

11. Ch. de Tolnay, 'Michelangelo Studies', *Art Bulletin*, September 1940, p. 130 ff.

12. A. Fişchel, *Raphael*, London 1948, p. 207 and *passim*.

13. W. Watzold in *Dürer's Befestigungslehre*, Berlin 1916, is of a different opinion.

E. Panofsky, *A. Dürer*, 2nd ed., Princeton 1948, I, p. 527, takes only a superficial interest in the architectural treatise. His reference to the 'Fuggerei', a settlement for poor citizens in Augsburg of *c.* 1519, is chronologically impossible, and its alignment of streets appears unrelated to Dürer's square and circular plans. Toy, *Fortification*, op. cit., p. 216 ff.

14. The interesting hypothesis of E. W. Palm with regard to a plan of Tenochtitlán stimulating Dürer's inspiration is not impossible, but the similarities are confined to the quadrangular plan as such, the function being entirely different. *Journal de la Société des Américanistes*, N.S. XL, 1951, p. 59 ff.

15. Sir Thomas More, *Utopia*, Louvain 1516.

16. M. L. Berneri, *Journey through Utopia*, London 1950, p. 58 ff.

17. A. von Martin, *Sociology of the Renaissance*, London 1944.

18. For a good survey of the problem, cf. W. Hager in *Festschrift Martin Wackernagel*, op. cit., p. 112 ff. G. Münter, *Idealstädte*, Berlin 1957 and *Die Geschichte der Idealstadt*, *Städtebau*, XXIV, 1929, pp. 249 ff. and 317 ff. S. Lang in *Architectural Review*, August 1952, p. 91 ff. F. Barbieri, *Vicenza*, Vicenza 1952, with special reference to Scamozzi. Brinckmann, *Stadtbaukunst*, op. cit., p. 40 ff.

    F. Chabod, *Machiavelli and the Renaissance*, London 1958, throws light on the ideology and aspirations of Machiavelli. It is interesting that the influence of *The Prince* on later absolute rulers finds its parallel in the influence of Mannerist planning during the 17th century.

19. N. von Holst, *Die Deutsche Bildnismalerei*, Strasburg 1930, especially p. 47. This study of German portraiture is revealing with regard to the general trends of taste. On iconography, cf. E. Panofsky, *Studies in Iconology*, New York 1939, especially p. 33 ff.

20. Numerous editions of Serlio's writings exist; the first and second books seem to have first appeared in 1545. W. B. Dinsmoor on Serlio in *Art Bulletin*, 1942, pp. 55 ff. and 115 ff. A. O. Lovejoy and G. Boas, *Primitivism and Related Ideas in Antiquity*, Baltimore 1935. T. E. Lawrenson in *Les Fêtes de la Renaissance*, I, p. 425 ff., and *The French Stage in the 17th Century*, Manchester 1957, *passim* and p. 14 f. H. Röttinger, *Die Holzschnitte zum Vitruvius Teutsch*, Strasburg 1914.

21. cf. R. Meiggs, *Roman Ostia*, Oxford 1960.

22. Lavedan II, p. 74 ff. and *passim*. R. E. Dickinson, *The West European City*, London 1951, gives a good although not exhaustive account. That the radial plan did not entirely supersede the grid-iron is seen in Gattinara, Valetta and Livorno, all of the 16th century. Hautecœur I, p. 586 f.

23. On Thélème, cf. Ch. Lenormant, *Rabelais et l'architecture de la Renaissance*, Paris 1840 (I owe this reference to Miss D. Thickett). cf. also J. Bédier and P. Hazard, *Histoire de la littérature française*, vol. I, *passim*. Rabelais, *Œuvres*, ed. A. Lefranc and others, Paris 1912, etc. cf. A. Blunt, *Philibert de l'Orme*, London 1958.

24. cf. note 20 above; Professor E. Heckscher emphasized in conversation the importance of this particular *entrée*.

25. On Andreae, cf. F. E. Held's introduction to *Christianopolis*, New York 1916.

26. Although the ramifications of military history in architecture cannot be studied here, a discussion of the influence of Mannerist town-planning on later periods will be found subsequently.

27. I owe this reference to Professor D. M. White.

28. cf. *Social Purpose*, *passim*.

29. That painting in turn influenced sculpture, especially relief, is only to be expected, but leads beyond the subject of this study.

30. J. Burckhardt, *The Civilisation of the Renaissance*, numerous editions. Also H. Wölfflin, *Principles of Art History*, New York 1950, and *Classic Art*, London 1952, op. cit.

31. Von Holst, op. cit., p. 47.

32. The literature on El Greco is extensive. cf. particularly A. L. Mayer, *El Greco*, Berlin 1931, *passim*. K. Pfister, *El Greco*, Vienna, Berlin, Zurich, 2nd ed. 1951, *passim*. The book by L. Goldscheider, first published in London in 1938, gives satisfactory reproductions, but the text fails to throw new light on the subject.

IV

The Age of the Baroque

European cities frequently received their main outlines and most imposing buildings during the Baroque period. This striking first impression is confirmed by the study of architectural design. The planned achievement, rather than the ideal plan, characterizes the age.[1] The 'embellishment' of particular quarters, resulting in huge avenues and straight vistas directed towards the most significant buildings, mainly churches and palaces, also exerted a formative influence. This can be seen clearly in Carlo Fontana's projected layout for the connecting avenue between Bernini's Piazza, in front of St Peter's Church in Rome, and the Tiber, or in the design of the town of Versailles, adjacent to the palace, mainly by J. Hardouin Mansart. The famous and abortive plan for the rebuilding of London in 1666 by Sir Christopher Wren also conforms to this pattern, and the designs for an alternative solution of the Piazza of St Peter's in Rome, published by Wittkower, are typical. Presumably because these were larger, and lacked the classical grandeur of Bernini, they, too, were rejected.[2]

From these familiar examples, regional developments in Europe were largely derived,[3] the emphasis shifting gradually from Italian to French prototypes, reflecting the evolution of political power. The embellishment of existing towns by emphasizing the axial element rather than the building of new cities is typical, and in this sense the Baroque is characterized by expansion rather than unfettered creation. This view of the axial element is corroborated by a study of contemporary coins, as they clearly illustrate projected and executed layouts and demonstrate the view-point to be adopted by the spectator.

It is significant that in Richelieu, the town and palace (designed by Jacques Lemercier at the behest of the Cardinal, and named after him) have no artistic unity: they are independent parts, connected only by the gardens, which contain a *patte d'oie*. Whilst it is possible that these gardens influenced the layout of those at Versailles, the part of the town of Versailles adjacent to the palace is modelled on a section of Rome, which includes the three famous streets laid out in the 17th century, meeting in what is called nowadays the Piazza del Popolo, and the churches of S. Maria dei Miracoli and S. Maria in Montesanto.

New editions and translations of Vitruvius, among them
Perrault's and Galiani's, achieved popularity in the 17th and
18th centuries.[4] The walls of his town plan were emphasized;
and the use of the sector as a formal element allowed for focal
points of especial religious or social interest. It favoured the
planning of a wide *place d'armes* which had existed previously
on a smaller scale in the Mannerist designs for fortifications,
but had never received such emphasis. Furthermore, the
buildings or avenues forming the boundaries of these sectors
could be extended *ad libitum*, thus opening up the countryside.

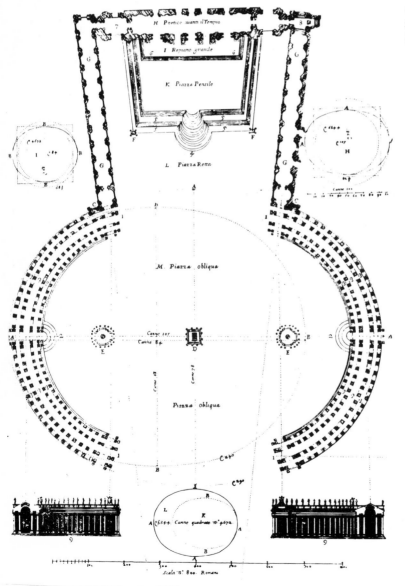

Ground-plan of the Piazza of St Peter's
in Rome; after Fontana's *Templo Vaticano*.
[See p. 71.]

Aerial view, showing the Palace and Town of Versailles. (By courtesy of Photo Direction Générale du Tourisme) [See p. 71.]

The Vitruvian influence is seen in Karlsruhe, a new capital for the Margrave Carl Willhelm of Baden, founded about 1715.[5] Here the sector is used for the city plan, whilst the **gardens complete the circle. Even the name of the streets** surrounding the castle are characteristically *Zirkel* ('circle').

It is easy to see that the two elements, the focal points and the expanding sectors of a fan-like design, were well fitted to express the ideology of the Baroque and the desire for political centralization. They were equally suited to provide the patterns for newly created or expanding towns, as the lack of a fixed boundary allowed for unlimited penetration of the country. The aureoles of clouds and the complicated spatial rhythms in church designs and pictorial ceilings, in palaces and garden patterns, were conducive to a similar stylistic expression, the illusion of extension.[6]

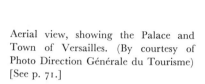

Medal showing a bird's-eye view of Karlsruhe. (By courtesy of the Badisches Landesmuseum)

Effects were produced in interior decoration by *trompe-l'œil* paintings and stucco decorations which gave an impression of spaciousness. These tendencies, apparent as early as the 15th century in the Camera dei Promessi Sposi by Mantegna in Mantua, culminated in the large perspectives of the Padre Pozzo in Rome, where realistic means are used to produce irrational effects – a method typical of the Counter-Reformation.

The term '*barocco*', which originally meant 'irregular', also characterized the ensuing style, the Rococo (derived from the irregular *rocaille*) and its allied style, leading to picturesque effects. The picturesque element should not be overstressed, however, especially in France. The underlying principles of unity and order were maintained and cogently pointed out in Descartes' well-known statements in the opening sentences of

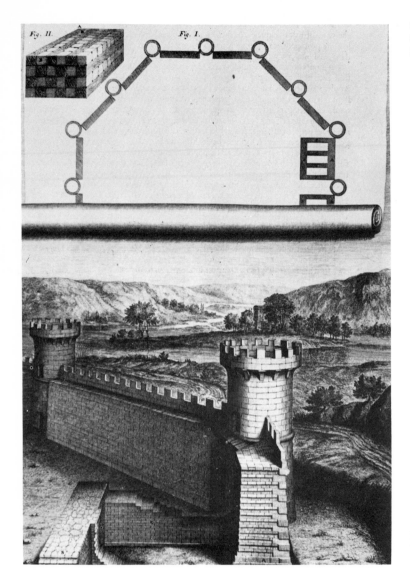

Ground-plan and view of Fortifications; from Perrault's *Vitruvius* (1st ed., 1673). [See p. 72.]

Diagram of the Town and Winds; from Perrault's *Vitruvius* (1st ed., 1673). [See p. 72.]

the second part of the *Discours de la méthode*, praising uniformity in plans and immediate execution in order to avoid irregularities and sudden changes:

'*Ainsi voit-on que les bâtiments qu'un seul architecte a entrepris et achevés ont coutume d'être plus beaux et mieux ordonnés que ceux que plusieurs ont tâché de raccommoder en faisant servir de vieilles murailles qui avaient été bâties à d'autres fins. Ainsi que ces anciennes cités qui, n'ayant été au commencement que des bourgades, sont devenues par succession de temps de grandes villes, sont ordinairement si mal compassées . . . on dirait que c'est plutôt la fortune, que la volonté de quelques hommes usant de raison, qui les a ainsi disposées.*'

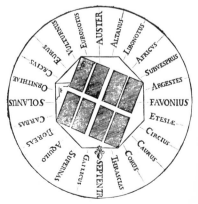

Hull, from an engraving by Hollar.

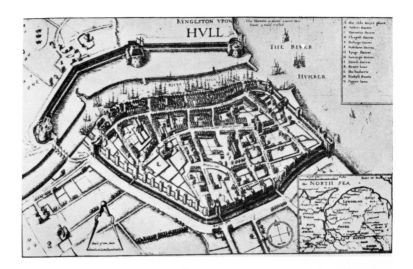

Relief plan of Spalato on the façade of the
Church of Santa Maria del Giglio.
(Photograph: Böhm)

A tendency to idealize counteracted the exactness desired in
topographic studies. Existing cities were subjected to a process
of design which regularized the streets and suggested a planned
and rational layout. For the art historian such designs are
useful, since they show with significant clarity the taste of the
period. Such developments have been traced by Professor Tout
in W. Hollar's engraving of Hull, for example.[7]

An outstanding example of interest in topography is seen in
the façade of the church of Santa Maria del Giglio or Zobenigo
in Venice, built between 1680 and 1683 by Giuseppe Benoni;
this shows in relief the outlines of the famous cities of Zara,
Padua, Rome, Corfu and Spalato, and the island of Crete.[8]

The sequence appears as a decorative element, of value for its own sake, and is based on the family history of the Benoni.

Vauban's fortifications may be regarded as new towns, since they make ample provision for accommodation. This can be seen in the rising manufacturing cities, for example Lille, and the new foundations, such as Neuf-Brisach. Lille, '*reine des citadelles*', retained its irregular medieval ground-plan, whilst Neuf-Brisach is octagonal in outline, with a central square. Vauban was indebted to the Mannerist tradition, but, surprisingly, his hornworks show strongly the influence of Michelangelo's bastions. On the other hand, Vauban's collaboration with Colbert, his insight into the development of forestry, the breeding of pigs and colonization, foreshadow the age of the Physiocrats, with their emphasis on agriculture.

Vauban's sympathy for the poor, the '*bas peuple, les pauvres gens*', his desire to find them useful work, combines a utilitarian with a humane interest, an attitude unusual among his contemporaries.[9] His fortified towns are telling examples of the attempted integration of all classes, the patterns being derived from the Mannerists, coupled with improved military techniques.

In the sphere of industrial building, the prevalent influence of 'the palace type' is apparent, for example in the factory and precincts of the van Robais family in Abbeville.[10] The director's dwellings are sumptuous, and then the employees and workers

Aerial view of Naarden, showing the Fortifications. (By courtesy of the Netherland Information Office)

are provided for on a diminishing scale, according to rank, including small individual cottages for the weavers.

The 17th-century fortifications of Holland, such as Naarden, are indebted to the Mannerists for their regularity and symmetry.[11] The same aesthetic approach is seen in Dutch architectural paintings, such as the church interiors by Saenredam, the prospect of Delft by Vermeer, or the views into open courtyards and alleyways by Pieter de Hoogh, giving a microcosmic and dignified view of the contemporary feminine world. In these works the elements of order, clarity and symmetry are stressed, at a time when the country was threatened by war, by economic competition from outside and the constant fight against the encroaching sea-water. In this contrast between reality and art, an anti-Baroque attitude verging on the Utopian is discernible in Holland. Conversely, the introspective mind of Rembrandt expressed itself frequently in forms based on the Italian Baroque, adding a mysterious character to his architectural backgrounds, which gave an individual and penetrating answer to the psychological and religious problems of his period.[12]

Characteristically, it was in this period that the regulations governing the height of buildings, their elevations and windows, were introduced, in order to realize a unified appearance, which would at the same time reflect the structure of society. The best-known example is probably the regulation applied to the rebuilding of London in 1667, which classed houses in four categories according to the number of storeys they had.[13] This type of regulation produces uniform street frontages, which create an effect similar to that of an ideal city, although the town centre as such does not come within its control. Perhaps no other feature is more characteristic of the Baroque town, based on empiricism, and the attempt to beautify the township as a whole.

The earliest instances of this type of planning are found in Holland, where the shortage of land and the planning of canals led to a wide adoption of regular plans and the control of building heights, standard plot frontages, and even regulations governing the bricks to be employed.[14] Here England seems to have followed in the wake of the Netherlands.

This is not the place to discuss German developments during the Baroque period, since empirical achievement rather than ideal planning dominated. But some of the designs are so grandiose in character that they belong among the best created in Europe, owing to the political and artistic ambitions of independent states and their rulers. Plans for Berlin, Munich, Schwetzingen, Ludwigslust and Würzburg are only a few of the examples which should be mentioned.

But even in Germany the Mannerist influence can be seen,

outstandingly so in Joseph Furttenbach's *Architectura Civilis*,
first published in Ulm in 1628, which shows different types of
house appropriate to various classes of society, all clearly
indebted to Italian and French influences. His small Lazaretto   Furttenbach, nos. 13, 39 and 40
and his large one are both based on the square, as is his cemetery
and many other schemes. He wished to isolate prisons from the
outside world, and planned schools of a quadrangular design,
with a chapel or library in the centre. Town halls, he thought,
should be placed in the city centre, and he suggested a combination of hostels and work places for artisans.

Furttenbach's *œuvre* included military and civic subjects,
private and recreational buildings, but he also suggested
solutions for garden planning proper, especially in his *Architectura Recreationis*, published in Augsburg in 1640. He prided
himself on his knowledge of Latin and Italian, and his wide
travels in Italy stood him in good stead.[15]

Baroque architecture was preponderantly axial and inclined
to express realistic and theatrical effects. Truth, in the sense
of functional use of materials, was sacrificed to appearance –
indeed no other age has succeeded in welding nature and
civilization so powerfully into an aesthetically satisfying unity.
This unity was based on a shrewd appraisal of the possible,
coupled with subservience to the way of life of royalty and the
aristocracy, and as close an imitation of it as the upper and
lower middle-classes could reasonably hope to achieve.

Interest in the new 'science' of history grew and culminated
in the work of J.-B. Vico (1665–1774). Earlier than this, we
find in England an appreciation of historical continuity. Sir
Christopher Wren was aware of the strength of the Gothic
tradition in England:

'I have found no little difficulty to bring Persons, of otherwise
a good Genius, to think anything in Architecture could be
better than what they had heard commended by others, and
what they had view'd themselves. Many good Gothick forms
of Cathedrals were to be seen in our Country.'

And so, Wren suggests, those who favoured the Classical
medium in architecture had to overcome traditional taste.

'I judge it not improper to endeavour to reform the Generality
to a truer taste in Architecture by giving a larger Idea of the
whole Art, beginning with the reasons and progress of it from
the most remote Antiquity.' (Quoted from the unpublished
Manuscript of the *Discourse on Architecture*.)[16]

It was on this basis that a widening of historical consciousness
was founded, creating a conception of architectural continuity

in contrast to the Renaissance approach which was basically oriented towards the Roman heritage. Wren's *Discourse on Architecture* and the *Tracts on Architecture* were unknown to Fischer von Erlach, since the former and the *Parentalia* were only published in 1750. But there can be no doubt that Wren profoundly influenced the historical conception of Sir John Vanbrugh (1664–1726), especially in the layout of Castle Howard and the turreted walls bordering its grounds. Horace Walpole, who developed this trend further, noted approvingly: 'But nobody . . . had informed me [in this connection] that I should . . . see a palace, a town, a fortified city . . .'[17]

Letter to A. G. Selwyn, 12 August 1772

Fischer von Erlach's *Entwurff einer historischen Architectur* of 1721 has also to be seen against this background.[18] This work was translated into French and later into English, but, significantly enough, not into Italian (though the French version was accessible to Italian *cognoscenti*). It forms a landmark in the evolution of historical thinking in the sphere of architecture. The author states in his preface that, in spite of changes of form, certain principles are maintained, such as symmetry, the structure of supports and loads, as well as the size of buildings and the orderliness of stone-work. But he is more interested in historical continuity, and suggests that buildings of the past can be regarded as inspirations for the future; in this sense, his concern for history also performs a practical function. Piranesi's historical concern with the Roman tradition and William Chambers's *Designs of Chinese Buildings* of 1757 are indebted to Fischer von Erlach's work: the latter had introduced models of Chinese design, and was the first writer to stress the sequence and magnificence of past architecture, using Villalpando's reconstruction of the Jewish Temple and including Greek and Roman prototypes in a broad survey. John Wood the Elder's theory, as expressed in *The Origin of Building* (Bath, 1741), stressing continuity and the pre-eminence of the Jewish temple, is also derived from him.

G.-B. Piranesi's (1720–78) visions of ancient Rome are characterized by heavy forms reminiscent of the Baroque. He was particularly interested in the tombs of the Via Appia and the Via Ardeatina, and found there, in the historical past, an inspiration for the present. For him, ancient Rome was truly an ideal city, which he reconstructed in his drawings and etchings representing *Le Antichità Romane*, first published in 1756.[19]

From the point of view of the ideal city, it is revealing how he included in detail the marble fragments of the *Forma Urbis Romae* and repeatedly gave a view of the Via Appia, showing huge funerary monuments, as well as obelisks and pyramids, as tokens of the great antiquity of Roman civilization. Presumably, Boullée's preference for Roman rather than Greek architecture

G.-B. Piranesi, Via Appia; from *Le Antichità Romane*

was stimulated by Piranesi, as the former does not seem to have visited Italy. Piranesi, essentially a Baroque artist born out of his period, thus forged a link between the Roman past and the Neo-Classicists, and also made an impact on the topographers and Romantics of the future.

It is no exaggeration to say that some of Piranesi's fantastic designs, especially the *Carceri*, so modern in character because they foreshadow a Utopia of horror and destruction, are still based on the Baroque tradition, but also link it with the present period, in its sombre 'existentialist' character. The conception of the evil city, derived from the Middle Ages, also lingers on here, showing how certain trends in European civilization persist, as it were *sotto voce*, in spite of changes of style and attitudes. Thus Piranesi's concern with historicity remains indebted to the Baroque.

In this period, a direct relationship between the image of the town and cosmic conceptions appears: thus the infinitesimal calculus can be paralleled with the large and extended avenues of Baroque townships. Whatever the value of such comparisons, the co-ordination of macrocosm and microcosm is illustrated by them. Slowly, however, the ideal image is replaced by an historical perspective and the consciousness of changing time. An art developed which lent itself to propaganda purposes, but which expressed wealth, power and opulence, rather than the aspirations of people of more humble status.

The attempts to show architectural continuity and the desire to reveal the underlying similarities of differing forms are connected with the development of historical studies in general, but also emphasize the unity of the world as experienced during the Baroque period and the appreciation of the time factor in human development, thus affording a parallel to the new conceptions of space, characteristic of the period.

Interest in the occult survives beneath rationalism, so the persistence of certain medieval patterns is not surprising. This led to a Gothic survival and revival, and to many new interpretations of ancient themes, either literally or in the spirit of the picturesque. The Tower of Babel, or the figure of the sun-god associated with Louis XIV, retained their symbolism of evil and good respectively.[20] The structure of the Tower of Babel, built up in a number of diminishing tiers, is directly reminiscent of the layout of either Dante's 'Inferno' or 'Purgatorio' in the *Divina Commedia*. The same subject is found earlier in a famous painting of 1563 by Pieter Brueghel, now in Vienna, and, following him, in the work of many lesser Baroque artists.[21] Campanella's City of the Sun was no doubt influenced in its basic conception by this image of the Tower of Babel, since it rises on the top of seven great concentric circles, which correspond to the seven planets. The walls are richly decorated with a survey of human achievement. In the centre is a circular temple, its altar decorated by a globe, reflecting in an eclectic manner the taste of the Renaissance, coupled with Platonic tradition and reminiscences of More's Utopia.[22]

For those artists who refused to be ruled by absolute political power and wished for solitude, voluntary exile from the splendours of the courts became a necessity; Poussin and Claude Lorraine, living isolated in Rome, were the most outstanding exponents of this attitude. They both integrated dreamy villages in an idealized landscape, but Poussin especially may be regarded as a planner, because of the thoughtful way in which his clearly conceived and regularly built houses form a significant foil for his Greco-Roman and Old Testament themes. For him the ideal town was part of the ideal landscape.[23]

In his painting of Eliezer and Rebecca in the Louvre, for example, the buildings which form the background and the setting are part of an ideal environment. They combine classical reminiscences with an emphasis on simple stereometric forms, such as the globe supported by a pillar, forming part of the well. Similarly, in the painting of the Ordination (now on loan to the National Gallery of Scotland in Edinburgh), a pillar is again significant, symbolizing the stone which stands for the Rock of the Church. Some individual buildings are meant to evoke Egyptian influences in Rome itself, based on the familiar pyramid of Cestius. In these two examples, the cities are ideal in that they represent no particular time or place, and are characterized by an austere dignity, which gives them a universal meaning. They are set in a landscape reminiscent of the Roman *campagna*, though no specific aspect is recalled.[24] Winckelmann is no stranger to this development, because his reinterpretation of Greece is based mainly on Roman sculpture and Roman prototypes.[25]

But this idealizing tendency is not the most characteristic of the age. Emphasis was on a humane utilitarianism, and on pleasing illusions, showing the unreal by realistic means. The fusion of the city and the landscape in the work of Poussin and to a lesser extent in that of Claude represents – although only marginally in its own period – a germinating factor for the future of planning.

To sum up: Mannerist tendencies remained a powerful element in the Baroque, but they were counteracted by an emphasis on the planning of independent city parts, which were combined with, or enhanced by, illusionistic effects. These developments, based on the rising power of centralized political forces, made use of varied historical reminiscences, but failed to involve those exiles who found in Italy the fulfilment of their artistic aspirations.

During this period the desire for architectural and illusionistic expansion was paradoxically coupled with emphasis on the partial plan, rather than development of the whole. 'Pars pro toto' might serve as the motto: a variety of parts regarded as units of possible expansion. The two planned cities of Versailles and Karlsruhe, with their fan-like designs, represent the main aspects of Baroque planning: the significance of the sector and the potential of unlimited expansion, combined with a rare emphasis on the unity of the entire town.

1. A. E. Brinckmann, *Stadtbaukunst*, Berlin-Potsdam 1920, is still best on town developments in the Baroque period.

2. E. Coudenhove-Erthal, *Carlo Fontana*, Vienna 1930, *passim*, especially p. 93 ff. On Versailles, cf. Lavedan II, *passim*. On Wren, cf. V. Fürst, *The Architecture of Sir Christopher Wren*, London 1956, p. 6 f., and E. F. Sekler, *Wren and his Place in European Architecture*, London 1956, p. 58 ff. cf. on the Baroque also E. A. Gutkind, *Revolution of Environment*, London 1946, p. 46 ff., and A. Blunt, *Art and Architecture in France*, London 1953. R. Wittkower in *Journal of the Warburg and Courtauld Institutes*, III, 1939–40, p. 88 ff.

3. H. Rose, *Spätbarock*, Munich 1922, *passim*.

4. cf. C. Perrault, *Les Dix Livres de Vitruve*, 2nd ed. Paris 1684. B. Galiani, *L'Architettura di M. Vitruvio Pollione*, Naples 1788.

5. On Karlsruhe, cf. K. Ehrenberg, *Baugeschichte von Karlsruhe*, Karlsruhe 1908. Also A. E. Brinckmann and L. Oelenheinz in *Zeitschrift für Bauwesen*, 1913, pp. 567 ff. and 603 ff., respectively.

6. E. Stadler in *Die Kunstformen des Barock-Zeitalters*, ed. R. Stamm, Berne 1956, gives a good survey of the different arts during the period concerned. An important and typical treatise is Father Andrea Pozzo's *Perspectiva Pictorum et Architectorum*, Rome 1693–1700.

7. cf. Tout, op. cit.

8. cf. A. E. Brinckmann, *Die Baukunst des 17. und 18. Jahrhunderts in den Romanischen Ländern*, Handbuch der Kunstwissenschaft, Berlin 1915, p. 110, fig. 116. The building itself is by G. Sardi. A paper by Jeanne Hugueney was given on the subject on the occasion of the XVIII International Congress of the History of Art in Venice in 1955.

9. R. Th. Blomfield, *Sébastien le Prestre de Vauban*, London 1938. P. Lazard, *Vauban*, Paris 1934. These works, however, throw little light on the relation between Michelangelo and Vauban.

10. A. Laprade, *Croquis*, I, Paris 1942, pl. 18.

11. The Dutch developments deserve special study, since the situation of this small country, struggling against political foes and the forces of the encroaching sea-water, demanded particular adaptations. As Wölfflin especially shows, Dutch art, when typical, is only Baroque in a limited manner. By contrast, even in such an introspective and individualistic artist as Rembrandt, certain Baroque features in the Italian sense are apparent. H. Wölfflin, *Principles of Art History*, English translation, London 1932.

   On Dutch architecture, cf. G. L. Burke, *The Making of Dutch Towns*, London 1956; especially on Denmark, S. E. Rasmussen, *Towns and Buildings*, Liverpool University Press, 1951.

12. O. Spengler, *The Decline of the West*, numerous editions, *passim*.

13. J. Summerson, *Georgian London*, London 1945, p. 36 ff.

14. cf. Burke, op. cit., p. 130. It is worth noting that the English 'area' below the street level is also indebted to Dutch prototypes, the Amsterdam *stoep* and its equivalent in other towns of Holland. cf. Rasmussen, op. cit., p. 92.

15. cf. also the idealizing elements in J. Furttenbach's *Newes Itinerarium Italiae*, Ulm 1627, as opposed to the more conventional designs by his famous contemporary, M. Merian.

16. Sekler, op. cit., p. 51.

17. L. Whistler, *Sir John Vanbrugh*, London 1938, and by the same author, *The Imagination of Vanbrugh and his Fellow Artists*, London 1954.

18. G. Kunoth, *Die Historische Architektur Fischers von Erlach*, Düsseldorf 1956, deals with the antecedents, but not future influences based on Fischer von Erlach.

19. cf. on Piranesi, H. Thomas, *The Drawings of G. B. Piranesi*, London 1954, with good bibliography. The Baroque character is emphasized by Piranesi's copies after Fischer von Erlach's themes. The outstanding monograph is still by H. Focillon, *G. B. Piranesi*, Paris 1918, p. 51 ff., and on influences in England, p. 300 ff. The influence of Piranesi's frontispiece of ancient Rome is seen in Erastus Salisbury Field's *Historical Monument of the American Republic, c.* 1875, reproduced by F. I. Jenkins in the *Journal of the R.I.B.A.*, 1958, p. 127. On Piranesi's change of style, cf. R. Wittkower in *Journal of the Warburg Institute*, 1938–9, p. 147 ff.

20. A. Parrot, *Ziggurats et Tour de Babel*, Paris 1949, *passim*. On the general problem, cf. J. Seznec, *La Survivance des dieux antiques*, London 1940.

21. cf. F. Grossman, *P. Bruegel, The Paintings*, London n.d., p. 194 f.

22. On Campanella, cf. L. Blanchet, *Campanella*, Paris 1920, especially p. 495 ff.

23. K. Gerstenberg, *Die Ideale Landschaftsmalerei*, Halle 1923, and *J. J. Winckelmann and A. R. Mengs*, Halle 1929.

24. F. S. Licht, *Die Entwicklung der Landschaft in den Werken von Nicolaus Poussin*, Basel 1954.

25. On Winckelmann, cf. W. Watzoldt, *J. J. Winckelmann*, 3rd ed. 1946, still the most comprehensive work on the man and his time. *Winckelmann und sein Jahrhundert*, ed. von Goethe, Tübingen 1805. Here the term 'heroic style' is used of Poussin, but Claude Lorraine is preferred. Winckelmann's love of freedom is expressed succinctly in a letter of 1754: '*Ich schwöre Dir, dass ich . . . dennoch die Freyheit aller Herrlichkeit der Welt vorziehen werde*' (p. 47).

Part Two

I

The Enlightenment in France

During the 18th century, two facts contributed to greater differentiation within the stratified European society, and to the growth of population: the industrial developments based on new machinery and the advances in agriculture. To these was added the growing power of the Third Estate, especially in France. Freedom of thought, represented by Voltaire and the *Encyclopédistes*, was paralleled by the need for new buildings for secular and civic purposes, whilst Rousseau's concern with nature had its impact on the design of gardens, and stimulated the effects of the picturesque.[1]

Planning was in advance of realization. Indeed, the transition from the Rococo to what is usually described as Neo-Classicism was slow, and became closely associated with a new functionalism.[2] This reflected the needs of the rising bourgeoisie, the desire of the monarchy's supporters to widen its popular appeal, and a partial recognition of the workers and peasants, the hitherto unacknowledged Fourth Estate. It was on this basis that the town-planners started to work.

The most important architectural document concerned with

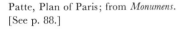

Patte, Plan of Paris; from *Monumens*.
[See p. 88.]

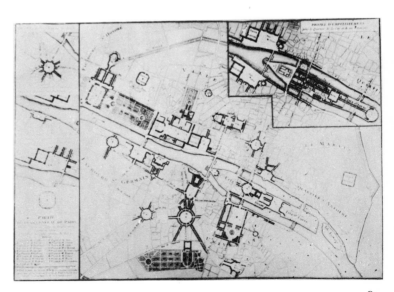

the changing consciousness of the period was the work of
Pierre Patte (1723–1814), who continued J.-F. Blondel's *Cours
d'architecture* from 1771 onwards, and shifted the emphasis from
buildings for the Court and nobility to the requirements of the
ordinary citizen.[3]

In spite of his long life, Patte's work was only effective when
he was about 40 years of age, since he possessed no resilience
and was unable to adjust to varying political circumstances.
He was also of a difficult temperament, which led to embittered
quarrels with Diderot. Nevertheless, he deserves wider recognition; in his treatise on *Monumens érigés à la gloire de Louis XV*,
first published in 1765, he combined a general literary survey
of the arts and a description of selected monuments to great
rulers and men, with a full account of the projects for the
monuments to King Louis XV, in Paris and in the provinces.
The King gave permission on 27 June 1748 for the Paris
venture to be begun; this led to a competition for differing
spatial solutions of the problem. He then decided to give the
site of the present Place de la Concorde for the purpose, and a
second competition followed, which was won by Ange-Jacques
Gabriel, who executed partial plans in 1752–53. This earliest
design for the now altered square already included a formal
architectural arrangement, as well as the combination with
the garden development along the river Seine. Patte assembled
these partial layouts on a master-plan which dealt with the
city as a whole, and thus produced what amounted to an ideal
plan of a multifocal city. Herein lies his particular and para-
digmatic contribution, since the multifocal principles gained
in importance with the passage of time.

Voltaire alluded to the replanning of Paris in a short essay
of 1749, 'Les embellissemens de Paris', and advocated radical
changes.[4] Paris, in order that it should be architecturally fit to
express its glory, was to be rebuilt by raising a special tax to
be levied on the citizens, on houses, or by other means. Voltaire
failed to enumerate, or to suggest, any architectural details,
being content to plead for beauty and representational dignity,
but his plea must be understood to be relevant to the plans for
the erection of statues to Louis XV in the squares of Paris and
in the provinces. It was with this background that Patte set to
work.

The variety of designs dealt with in the third part of Patte's
Monumens pays special regard to the amelioration of life within
the city, raising, among other problems, the question of the
preservation of ancient churches, which he did not propose to
destroy altogether. He wished to adapt Notre-Dame as a parish
church, but advocated a contemporary structure for a new
cathedral. He deprecated what he called 'cold symmetry' and
stressed the importance of street openings with easy accessi-

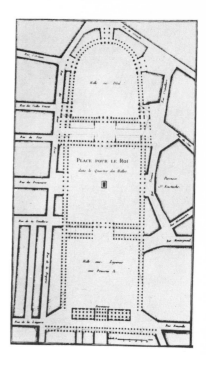

Boffrand, Plan of connected Markets;
from Patte's *Monumens*.

bility, which is related to his concern with '*convenance*'.

Patte's own redevelopment plan for Paris included the unification of the Isle St Louis with the Isle du Palais, and on this newly won terrain the new cathedral was to be placed. A building, symmetrical with regard to the ancient part of the Louvre, was to be erected on the opposite bank of the Seine; its purpose was to provide a palace for the *Parlement* or Law Courts, as well as prisons.

Patte, *Monumens*, plates XLV and XLVI

From the social point of view, Boffrand's designs for the markets are the most revealing, with their detailed arrangements of halls for selling vegetables and other commodities. These cater for the material desires of all classes, whilst the plan by Contant d'Ivry, including a project for the reconstruction of the Town Hall, gives an indication of the rise of civic pride and responsibility during the last stages of the French Monarchy.

Monumens, plates LI and LII

Formal emphasis on wide avenues and the continuation of the Vitruvian tradition are found in a circular development plan of 1752 for the region of the Rue de Bussi by P. N. Rousset. Here it is the formal, rather than the social, element which is dominant. From examples of this type the later developments of the Place de l'Étoile in the 19th century are derived. Similar in spirit is a design by Servandoni for a new square outside the city proper: a significant example of town extension. A broad outlook on education is expressed in Patte's description of free university courses.

Monumens, pp. 205 ff. and 210 ff.

Monumens, p. 67

Patte's ideas on town-planning are more explicitly stated in his *Mémoires sur les objects les plus importans de l'architecture* of 1769, where he demands the replacement of fortifications by four rows of trees, two bordering the central carriageway, the others flanking paths for pedestrians at the side. He is partial to removable awnings, which can be pulled out in inclement weather, and shows great concern for sanitary arrangements. The young architect, following in his footsteps, is warned against disappointment and frustration, no doubt the outcome of his own bitter experiences with Diderot and others.[5]

Rousset, Plan for a Circus on the Rue de Bussi; from Patte's *Monumens*.

In order to realize the importance of Patte's survey, it is essential to examine some of the squares executed in Paris and the provinces. However different they may appear in shape – octagonal, like the Place du Roi, now Place de la Concorde in Paris, varied in outline, as in the sequence of piazzas in Nancy, or rectangular like the original Places Royales in Bordeaux, Reims and Rouen – they are all of moderate size, which gives the passer-by a feeling of harmonious enclosure and leisurely ease.

This is particularly apparent in the Place Royale, now Place de la Bourse, in Bordeaux, begun by Jacques Gabriel in 1733. It is situated on the river Garonne, without, however, incorporating the main visual effect of the winding stream.

Two symmetrical buildings emphasize the enclosure at the sides and the circumscribed vista of the river. As far as possible, the arrangement is static, reminiscent of a lakeside view. A similar effect within the town was achieved in Reims by Le Gendre after 1756, and in Rouen by Le Carpentier after 1757. Here the vertical outlines of the Cathedral and the Church of St Ouen enhance the horizontal elevations of the municipal buildings, and express their qualities of enclosure.

View of the Place de la Bourse, Bordeaux.

The static effect was stressed by centrally placed statues, among which the one of Louis XV in Reims is outstanding. On its socle are two symbolic figures, one female, gently leading a lion and expressing Peaceful Government, the other male, representing the Happy Citizen; this nude figure, seated on a sack of goods, with money falling from a purse, is accompanied by a lamb and wolf lying peacefully together. The Citizen, sometimes considered to be the sculptor's portrait, is treated as realistically as Pigalle's nude model for Voltaire, and represents the common people, their work and dignity. The statue, about which a letter from the sculptor to Voltaire exists,[6] stands for a new departure in European evolution, which culminated in the 'Miners' of Meunier and the 'Thinker' of Rodin.

The monument, executed after 1762, expresses the spirit of the Age of Enlightenment, since the standing figure of the king is of less significance then the allegorical representations on the socle. The general admiration was not, however, shared by Diderot; he, as the protagonist of an almost unmitigated – although sentimental – realism, complained in the Salon of 1765 that the Citizen, in the guise of a figure in the nude and seated on a sack, was quite unsuitable for expressing security in the reign of Louis XV. He especially criticized the nude as being inappropriate for a northern climate, since even during the hottest weather in France, unlike in Greece and Italy, the inhabitants would not think of shedding their clothes. He therefore demanded that common sense should be used in devising a suitable costume. This criticism merits emphasis as it illustrates the prevalent trend towards realistic taste at that time.[7]

Père Laugier, in his *Essai sur l'architecture*, first published in 1753 and reissued in 1755, expressed a similar spirit.[8] He was concerned with the comfort rather than the splendour of dwellings, which should be fitted to the social rank of the inhabitants. He appears in this context as an early functionalist: function to be based on content and create form. He pointed out that bedrooms should not be situated on top of one another, and that kings and princes would, for that reason, be suitably lodged in single-storey buildings, an idea which had earlier occurred to King Frederick II of Prussia when building Sans-Souci in 1744–47.

Laugier, *Essai* (2nd ed.), p. 152 f.

Essai (2nd ed.), V. *De l'embellissement des villes*, p. 209

Observations sur l'architecture, The Hague, 1765, p. 313

On the entrances to cities, cf. *Essai*, V

According to Laugier, hospitals should show that they were intended for the poor, and thus express simplicity and restraint, but the rich were enjoined to practise moderation as well; these precepts were similar to those already found in Alberti's writings. Laugier was in favour of straight, planned streets, like roads in a forest, ending in triumphal arches, and deplored capricious and overstressed ornament: '*Ce goût . . . doit s'étendre aux Villes entières . . . On bâtit de nouvelles maisons: mais on ne change ni la mauvaise distribution des rues, ni l'inégalité difforme des décorations faites au hasard et selon le caprice de chacun.*' Similar points are made in his *Observations sur l'architecture*: '*Le plan de Paris a été fait au hasard et sans dessein . . . C'est une grande forêt pleine de routes et de sentiers, tracés sans méthode.*' Here Laugier's appraisal is entirely that of the Classicist, although his attitude towards the orders, especially pilasters and arcades, was unusually negative.

In Morelly's *Code de la nature*, published in 1755, a communist doctrine of a hieratic order, based on a mathematical concept of equality, but graded according to age and sex, was realized in multiples and division of 10 citizens – thus according with the decimal system. Acquisition of goods was to be free, without the passing of money, since, for Morelly, financial inequality was the source of all evil. In the fourth part of his treatise, dealing with legislation, certain ideas on town-planning are implied. The main square was to be surrounded by public buildings; regularity of siting and streets was demanded; and hospitals were to be provided outside the cities, following the tradition set by Alberti. Sterile parts of the country were to be fed by the neighbouring districts. Morelly's moral precepts, which were based on a Republican point of view, were to be enforced by Draconic legislation, which extended to the right of divorce and the communal upbringing of children. In Morelly, a new concern with the happiness and social conditions of the nation as a whole is allied to a strong Renaissance tradition of aesthetic regularity. He thus forms an important link between the town-planners and the social reformers.

The next step in the evolution of architectural taste in planning is found in M.-J. Peyre's (1730–88) publication of architectural designs in *Œuvres d'architecture* of 1765. These were intended to imitate and emulate the buildings erected during the Roman Empire, herein differing from Piranesi, who reconstructed the antique heritage in a spirit of Romanticism, imbued with a rather dilettante, but intuitive, archaeology.

Numerous designs by Peyre are found in the Bibliothèque Nationale and the Library of the École des Beaux-Arts in Paris. In his *Œuvres*, Peyre started by considering the individual site and isolated buildings; but he also dealt with larger, comprehensive units, of which the circular scheme including a

Cathedral flanked by two palaces, and the Academy with adjoining buildings, are outstanding.[9] The former was presented to the Accademia di S. Lucca in Rome in 1753; the latter is undated.

It is characteristic that the publication, a telling example of the emergence of the new functional style during the Rococo,[10] was dedicated to the Marquis de Marigny, brother of Madame de Pompadour. Peyre exerted a strong influence on his successors, among them Boullée especially, whose circular buildings, for example, continue the tradition set in the 'Sepulchral Chapel', which in turn is based on the '*Tour de Mételle*', the tomb of Cecilia Metella on the Via Appia. Any influence from Piranesi is thus confined to the subject matter, and has no stylistic significance.

Peyre, *Œuvres*, plates 5 and 6

In J.-F. Sobry's *De l'architecture*, published in 1776 in Amsterdam, the influence of the commercial classes as patrons of architecture makes itself felt: '*Si le maître de la Maison est homme d'affaire ou de négoce, vous disposerez . . . des chambres à recevoir, des bureaux ou des magasins.*' Sobry also realized the importance of the members of the socially lower strata, apparently for the first time in French architectural theory. He took an interest in the inhabitants of lodging houses, for whom he demanded large staircases and windows, high ceilings and good drainage: '*Les Maisons communes sont celles que les citoyens riches font bâtir dans les villes, pour bailler à d'autres, et pour en tirer du revenu.*' . . . '*Que les Maisons, destinées à servir de logement à plusieurs familles, soient bien percées et bien airées . . .*' '*Les citoyens opulens, à qui appartiennent les Maisons communes, et leurs architectes, doivent avoir ces attentions pour les familles inférieures.*' Thus architectural layout and social tendencies are clearly interlinked and objectively formulated.[11]

Sobry, *De l'architecture*, p. 170 ff.

It will be seen from the development sketched here, that a new approach to city planning is characteristic of the Age of Enlightenment, a development which in many ways is a break with the past, although formal continuity is maintained and Vitruvius is still regarded as the teacher, if not so much in practice, then at least in theory. What is new is a purely functional approach to '*commodité*' and progress, concepts now applied to the dwellings of the whole nation, rather than to the privileged classes alone.

Dupuis, Syncretistic View of World Religions; from *Origine de tous les cultes*.

The desire for classification and generalization, characteristic of the 18th century, was introduced into natural science in 1753 by Buffon in his '*dessein primitif et général*', which concerns animals. In the sphere of religion, a similar attitude is found in C. F. Dupuis's *Origine de tous les cultes*, first published in 1795, although the idea behind the work originated about 20 years earlier. Here the deities of various known religions are derived from differing interpretations and personifications of the con-

stellations and natural phenomena. Dupuis's comprehensive view is clearly expressed in the frontispiece of his work which shows figures of Egyptian and Greek mythology, among them Zeus, a bull piercing the cosmic egg, and pyramids. Architectural details in ruins counterbalance the figure of Mithras at the bottom, whilst Judaism is represented by the High Priest as well as the traditional lampstand with seven branches, and idolatry by the golden calf. The apex is formed by the Madonna and Child with Evangelists' symbols.

Condorcet attempted to describe historical progress in the sciences and the arts, but with some misgivings about the latter. He realized that taste changes, but being unaware of contemporary architectural inspiration, he could only hope that the current 'feebleness' of the arts would pass, and lead the way to a progress which would maintain appreciation of the best works of the past, and lead to the attainment of ever-improving standards by destroying prejudice.[12]

In Patte's *Monumens*, a comparable attempt at universality is made. Just as Buffon and Dupuis influenced future generations, so Patte's suggestions were taken up by the Classical Reformers, Boullée and Ledoux. Through their work, this attitude spread through Europe, and influenced city design in theory and practice.[12]

The Classical Reformers: Boullée and Ledoux

The late Dr Kaufmann, who did so much to foster comprehension and enthusiasm for 'Architecture in the Age of Reason',[13] in one of his earlier works coined the term 'autonomous' for this architectural style.[14] He is almost as mistaken as Sedlmayr, who blames the period for a lack of balance.[15] A novel social purpose, based on interest in the life of the common people, was encouraged and stimulated by the leading architects of the period, especially by Boullée (1728–99) and Ledoux (1736–1806), who can therefore be aptly described as 'Classical Reformers'. Avoiding the superfluous, they substituted a sense of austerity, an appeal to the essential and a distrust of ornament; they were opposed to the traditional idiom of the Rococo, thus facilitating the arrival of Classicism in the Empire style, as fostered by Quatremère de Quincy.[16] Boullée's important treatise, *Architecture, Essai sur l'art*, left by him to the Bibliothèque Nationale and only recently published,[17] reflected the writer's ideas from the pre-Revolutionary period to the year of his death in 1799. This work is characterized by two seemingly contradictory, but in reality supplementary, points of view. In his designs and descriptions of the Newton Cenotaph, for example, he represents a regular finite world, a globe – a form at present familiar in atomic reactors. On the other hand, in his thoughts about the immensity and infinity of nature, as well as in his concern for human relationships, Boullée transcends the limits of his time. He stands for a modern interpretation of the co-ordination of the diverse aspects of human knowledge. A static view of the world is superseded by a dynamic one, the finite by the infinite. His theory of symmetry may be regarded as the fulfilment of the Renaissance view of art, as well as the precursor of the expanding conceptions of variety in nature gravitating towards symmetry, which characterize our own time.[18]

In each instance Boullée asks himself what is the function of any particular work of architecture, a term which for him includes its concrete uses as well as its appeal to the emotions induced by structure, light and shadow. His idea of nature is thus not 'naturalistic' in a modern sense. It is ordered immensity which appeals to him, expressing the Newtonian finite world and transcending it by stressing the variety and dimension of the universe. He develops from the ornate to the simple; from alternating domes and open spaces, as in the 'Museum' and first 'Royal Library' schemes, to an austere and simple monumentality. Surveying his work, it cannot be denied that from the Hôtel Brunoy of 1762, the Cathedral of 1782, to the Newton Memorial of 1784, the façade of the Library of 1788 and the Palais Municipal of 1792, one finds a steady enlargement of vision, a broadening of social consciousness and a reduction of forms to their essential elements. As in the case of Michelangelo, Rembrandt, or Goethe, his artistic powers were undiminished with old age. If the greatness of a work of art is based on the depth and the universality of its appeal, then a significant place cannot be denied to Boullée.[19]

His large drawings of monumental buildings, sometimes set in an ideal landscape, are reminiscent of Poussin, and indeed, as a young man, Boullée had wished to become a painter rather than an architect. His numerous designs for individual buildings were intended to be part of a comprehensive scheme, including the city walls and gates, theatres, libraries, and buildings for communal use, such as museums and palaces of justice. He also designed a circular opera-house, set against a variety of backgrounds, among them one showing an Italianate townscape.[20] An adaptation of the Palace of Versailles to Republican needs is typical of his attitude, which was centred on civic dignity and a responsible way of life. However much his designs may differ in detail, they share an emphasis on simplicity, symmetry and monumentality, and have no superfluous ornament. Since Boullée wished to express the lasting and universal character of buildings serving a collective aim and appealing to the emotions, he was equally interested in

Boullée, City of the Dead set in an Ideal Landscape. (By courtesy of the Bibliothèque Nationale, Paris)

Boullée, Project for a City Wall. (By courtesy of the Bibliothèque Nationale, Paris)

Boullée, Project for an Opera House. (By courtesy of the Bibliothèque Nationale, Paris)

projects for civic centres and cemeteries; for him the individual and transient was secondary to the true purpose of architecture. For this reason, the grandiose views of cities for the dead, with their monumental walls and simple buildings, form an important element in his work.

Boullée's wish to erect his Cathedral on the Mont Valérien near Suresnes, or on Montmartre, where the Sacré-Cœur was begun in 1876, is an interesting example of decentralization and the development of multifocal planning.

Boullée, *Architecture*, p. 39

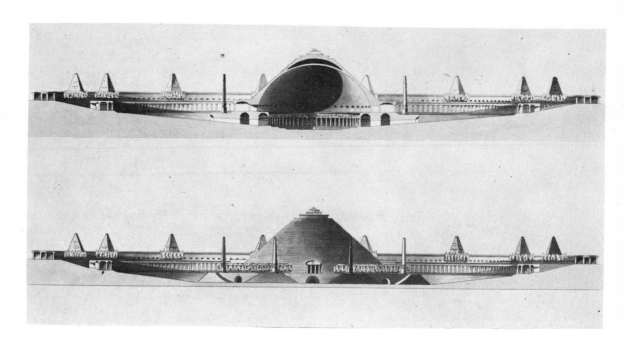

Fontaine, Designs for a Cenotaph; from Prieur (1785).

Since Boullée held an authoritative position as a member of the Academy of Architecture from 1762, his influence on the competition for the Rome prize is not unexpected. His project for the Cenotaph for Newton, of 1784, was the basis for the competition of 1785. A series of drawings by the master exists on this scheme; one dated 1784 is a fully finished design, but some of the others are more experimental. The first prize was allotted to Moreau, and the second prize to Fontaine (Prieur). The tradition continues in designs on the same subject by Gay in 1800 (*Projets*), Ledoux's 'Hoopmaker's House', Lequeu's 'Palace of Justice' and his '*Temple de la Sagesse Suprême*', to give only a few random examples.[21]

Boullée demanded a master plan for Paris, to be sponsored by the Academy, and in which – he may have hoped – his own buildings could find an appropriate place. Furthermore, he wanted plans of the large towns in the provinces to be designed, to facilitate open competition between architects. The outcome of these endeavours was Verniquet's plan of Paris after 1783, and the *Plan des Artistes* for the future city, commissioned on 1 and 4 April 1793. The latter, a comprehensive development plan, was unfortunately destroyed by a fire in the Paris Town Hall during the Commune of 1871, but the design was studied and reconstructed by Bernard in 1888 and critically evalued by Bardet. It is significant, and illustrative of the far-reaching historical influence of the period, that the *Plan des Artistes* has provided the basic design for the rebuilding of Paris.[22]

In spite of Boullée's radical views on art, he was suspect to

Boullée, *Architecture*, p. 91

the Revolutionaries, and was rightly regarded as a Royalist, although he escaped persecution. His work is akin to, and expressive of, the ideals of his age, though it also shows an interest in collective values unusual for his time.

Boullée was inspired by a clear conception of the universe, by the beauty of simple stereometric forms from which he deduced his ideas on more technical subjects, such as the painter's approach to symmetry and light and shadow. He wished to express immensity, eternity and the infinite through symbolic spheres; this is best seen in his Cenotaph for Newton, which forms a contrast to the spherical Hoopmaker's House by Ledoux, for example; this house, with its internal opening, is no more than a playful form with no specific relationship to its function. Boullée's approach throughout is that of a visionary, whilst Ledoux remains far more a practical architect. In fact, when Ledoux loses his empirical background, as in his designs for the cemetery of Chaux, he seems to adapt Boullée's conceptions to a Palladian style.[23] Boullée's National and Municipal Palaces, the prototypes of community centres, incorporate many of the ideas which Ledoux expanded frequently at a later date in a conventional form, as for instance in his 'Oikema', a brothel-like institution, in which bath and separate rooms lead to an elliptical hall, devoted to the teaching of morals; this idea is similar to Filarete's project for a house of vice and virtue, although certainly not connected with it, since Filarete was forgotten in France at that time – and, for that matter, in Italy, too. In contrast to this, Ledoux's 'Temple of Memory dedicated to the Virtue of Women' is more conventional in form and content, emphasizing the square block, to which four minaret-like turrets are added. More interesting are the 'Panarétéon', with its step-like approach to the central cube, and the 'Pacifère' or Temple of Conciliation, showing the same basic form, with the addition of fasces and inscribed slabs. 'Les principales maximes des moralistes anciens et modernes; les noms des Socrate, des Platon, des Marc-Aurèle, seront inscrits en lettres d'or.'

Certain Egyptian forms, obelisks and pyramids, had been in vogue from the Renaissance onwards to denote Antiquity; they were used for ceremonial occasions, or because of their emotional associations.[24] Boullée favoured them for cemeteries, since their austerity and lack of decoration suggested timelessness. But it was left to Ledoux to discover a functional use for the pyramids, as the furnaces for a forge, thus revealing again his gift for adapting forms to original functions. Indeed, these furnaces appear appropriate: they appeal by their simplicity, and their compact outline expresses solidity and allows for the necessary flues.[25] Pyramids remained popular as funerary monuments; one example is the structure in the centre of the market-place in Karlsruhe, by Weinbrenner in 1825, which

Ledoux, *L'Architecture*, p. 114

commemorates the Grand Duke Carl Wilhelm.

Boullée's originality and the impact of his work are borne out by his influence on Fontaine's project of 1785 for a Cenotaph, Gasse's projects for a cemetery of 1799, and Gay's and Labadie's designs for a Cenotaph for Newton, both of 1800, the last three of which form part of the *Projets*. Lequeu's drawings for a circular Temple of Justice are equally indebted to Boullée, as well as the plans for a National Library in the Luxembourg Palace by A.-M. Peyre, which develop the theme of Boullée's '*Bibliothèque Nationale*'.

It would be interesting to know more about the work of Bernard Poyet (1742–1824), architect to King Louis XVI and the City of Paris, who is well known for his colonnade in front of the Chambre des Députés in Paris. He wrote numerous pamphlets, including one, dated about 1790, on a Place de la Nation, that is, the re-planning of the centre of the capital near the Louvre. The scheme was to employ 40,000 artists and workers, and included public buildings, and 114 many-storeyed houses, some adorned with giant colonnades supporting terraced private and communal gardens. (The gardens on the upper storey foreshadow present-day trends.) Incidentally, Poyet rejected ideas for a circular opera-house which Boullée favoured.

Even such utilitarian buildings as the factory of Le Creusot, founded in 1782, with its decorative railway lines intended to lighten the burdens of dray horses, succumbed to the ornamental tradition.[26]

The concern of the period with education, town-planning and the integration of allegorical sculpture with architecture was

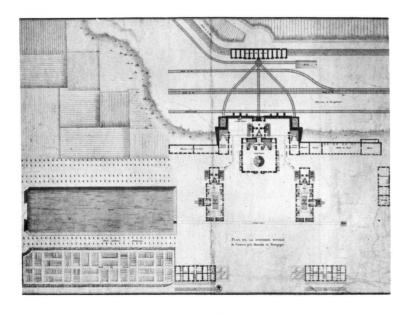

Le Creusot, layout of the Royal Foundry. (By courtesy of the Bibliothèque Nationale, Paris)

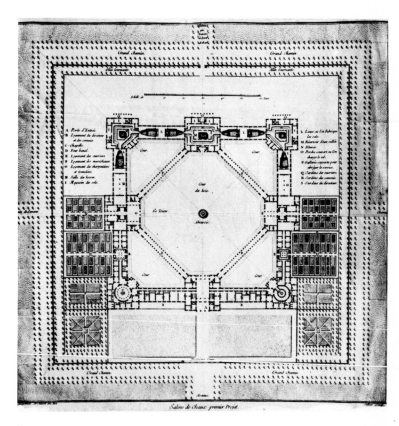

Ledoux, quadrangular Design for Chaux; from *L'Architecture*.
[See p. 100.]

intense; it applied, for instance, to the law passed by the National Assembly on 27 June 1792, regarding the 'Monument to Liberty' in the Place de la Bastille, and to the order of the Committee of Public Safety for the erection of a National Palace on the 25th Floréal, in the second year of the Republic.[27]

It is not surprising that in this atmosphere C.-N. Ledoux also toyed with Revolutionary architectural ideas, though he remained politically a Royalist. He gained fame through the publication of his *Architecture* in 1804, but shows a strong if unacknowledged debt to Boullée, as in his central Hoopmaker's House or his cube-like '*Panaréteon*', both mentioned above.

In the town-planning of the late 18th century two contradictory tendencies are apparent. Boullée designed clearly contained units; the *enceinte*, with its walls, is stressed in his text as well as in his drawings. He also formulated a clear structural programme, in which social and collective considerations are conspicuous, best seen in his series of palaces of a civic nature. But when the toll-houses and gates of Paris, built by Ledoux between 1785 and 1789, fell into disuse after 1791, this was celebrated as progress and an occasion for rejoicing. The revolutionary tenet of liberation, related economically to the freeing of trade, seemed at the time a panacea for all evils.

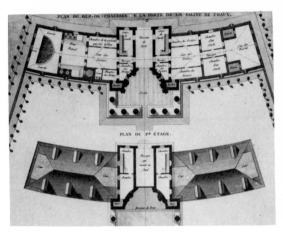

Ledoux's plans for Chaux, which located important buildings on an outer ring and included isolated houses and villages in the countryside, showed a similar tendency – towards the open plan. During the same period, several new towns or villages were planned, such as Carouge and Versoix near Geneva.[28] Ledoux's Chaux is only one such project.

In his first quadrangular design for Chaux, based on the Mannerist tradition and presumably transmitted by Iaques Perret, a well takes the place of the tower. The worker is newly considered an important and active factor in, and agent of, society. In earlier phases, for example the Fuggerei of *c.* 1519 intended for the poorer citizens in Augsburg, with its grid layout, the workers were regarded as passive recipients, and this was still true of Colbert's new industrial cities of the 17th

Above left
Ledoux, elliptical Design for Chaux; from *L'Architecture*.

Above right
Ledoux, projected Gate for Chaux, with Guardrooms and Living Quarters; from *L'Architecture*.

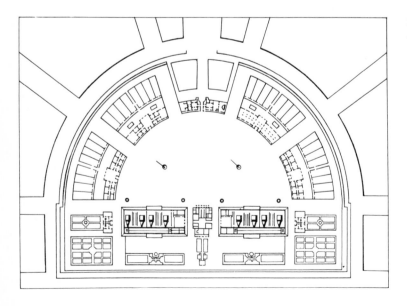

Ledoux, abbreviated Design for Chaux; after *L'Architecture*.

century, where cursory regard only was paid to the workers' needs and tastes.

The second plan for Chaux, Ledoux's 'ideal city', is elliptic, not circular, as frequently stated. It can be explained by visualizing the Vitruvian town layout coupled with the ground-plan of the Colosseum or the Piazza of St Peter's in Rome. The plan shows radiating avenues as well as a 'green belt' of trees which replaces the city walls and marks the city boundaries. It is typically ambivalent in this respect, representing a balance between the open and enclosed town. Among the outstanding features of Chaux are the separate traffic lanes, which leave the residential quarters undisturbed, and concentrate on the main arteries, thus opening up the countryside; furthermore, a ring road is added, giving an effect of spacial unity.

A partial and abbreviated design, based on a semi-circle, should be considered in conjunction with the two comprehensive plans of Chaux; it is similar to the second, roughly halving it, whilst retaining the commanding position of the salt works and adding prisons at the entrance gate.

The greatest merit of the plans of Chaux, and the point at which they made their specific contribution, was in their flexibility, and the design of a closed green belt, with only the main artery leading into the countryside. Although the individual houses are Palladian, and not particularly distinguished, their setting in the landscape is disposed with consummate skill. If it is true that static dispositions are characteristic of most earlier periods, then Ledoux may be regarded as the first modern architect, consciously introducing a dynamic element into his plans, whilst retaining the town centre.

In Ledoux's Chaux, one important aspect was the growing consideration for the rising Fourth Estate; a special community centre was to be constructed, while, as was customary at the time, each family was to be provided with an individual room. Referring to 'bâtiments destinés aux ouvriers', Ledoux said: 'Chaque chambre est occupée par une famille; une galerie aboutit à un foyer commun.' It was in this central kitchen that the cooking was done. Allotments provided for relaxation and no distractions were to vitiate the temper of the workers.

Whilst Boullée was in favour of a town appearing frankly as such, the 'garden city' aspect, revealed by Ledoux, was also to be found in the revolutionary Babeuf. The latter wanted large towns to disappear in order to replace them with villages 'ornés d'une immensité d'habitants heureux'.[29] But Boullée's emphasis on the walls of the town drew attention to the importance of the enceinte, or circumvallation. This notion was perhaps most succinctly expressed by Sobry in his treatise on architecture mentioned above: 'une ville sans mur n'est pas une ville'. Furthermore, Sobry disliked building on the periphery which left the

Ledoux, L'Architecture, plate 38

Sobry, De l'architecture, p. 150 ff.

centre empty. A greater contrast than that of Ledoux's second
plan for Chaux, an open garden city, can hardly be conceived.
There the dispersal of buildings on the outer oval is noticeable,
whilst in Boullée's work the accent is on the centre. His emphasis
on the enclosed town has a modern note, now that sprawling
suburbs are the planner's nightmare.

From Ledoux's oval surrounding Chaux to the *Ringstrassen*,
such as those found in 19th-century Vienna, it is expansion
beyond the boundary rather than the boundary itself which
influences design. The 'ring' acts not as an enclosure but as a
stimulus for expansion. The *enceinte* had become out of date
in the military sense in Boullée's time. It was, as his text shows,

An allegorical print of *c.* 1791, showing
the imminent destruction of the Paris
Toll Gates. (By courtesy of the Bibliothèque Nationale, Paris)

introduced for 'variety's sake', which meant for symbolic
reasons. Sobry, in his *Poétique des arts*, published in 1810, went
even further. He saw the symbolic meaning of the enclosing
town gates and walls: '*En passant sous les linteaux de la porte d'une
ville, on sent qu'on se soumet à ses lois.*'

Sobry was in advance of his time in recognizing the importance and adaptability of an old tradition. Popular sentiment
swayed in the opposite direction: when the toll enclosures of
Paris, which had only recently been completed by Ledoux,
were discarded on 1 May 1791, this led to great rejoicing. The
occasion was commemorated by an anonymous print with an
allegory of '*Le Mai des Français, ou les Entrées Libres*', with
Freedom destroying the barriers and Mercury, the god of
commerce, holding the centre.[30] The future repercussions of
the opening of towns, the removal of boundaries, and eventu-

Boullée, *Architecture*, p. 86

Sobry, *Poétique*, p. 413 ff.

ally the dangers of suburban sprawl, could hardly be appreciated at the time.

The Revolution appeared at first to encourage new commissions by the State of secular buildings of a civic and democratic, as against a royal, character. At the same time, the tendencies towards planning and centralization which had existed during the *Ancien Régime* were expected to continue. These contradictory hopes proved abortive. The Revolution failed to carry out the progressive plans envisaged by the painter J.-L. David and other contemporary artists.[31] In painting, this led to the individualistic bourgeois realism of the 19th century. As to sculpture, F. H. Dowley[32] comments on d'Angivillier's commissions for statues of great men, the first of which were exhibited in the Salon of 1777. In architecture, the development of the Hosten Estate of 1792 by Ledoux became the prototype for capitalist land development, leading eventually to the Boulevards of Haussmann.[33] The nobility was crushed and the power of capital finance increased, as one can see from builders' speculations: the Hosten Estate, for example, included a house of four storeys, easily subdivided into what at the present time are called 'maisonettes', with the ground and first floors, and the second and third floors respectively, forming complete residential units with separate kitchens. Equally remarkable is the plan for the park of the Hosten Estate, published in the second volume of Ledoux's *Architecture*. Here one finds a rectangular frame for the layout as a whole; two irregular circuses constitute private gardens, and a river winds through the estate. A school, planned by Ledoux, also emphasizes the park background with children playing. Certain influences derived from the English landscape garden may be traced in these arrangements, but the main outline of the designs remains within the French tradition of regularity.

Whereas at an earlier period royal palaces influenced the more utilitarian buildings of the nobility and the bourgeoisie, now artistic movements worked in the opposite direction. As has been explained by Ledoux in his *Architecture*, the late 18th century favoured simplicity, austerity and the suppression of unnecessary ornament. Accordingly, proportion and layout gained in importance, while decoration was either suppressed to an ever-increasing degree or omitted entirely.

'*Si l'art ne peut offrir aux uns* [the poor] *qu'une habitation modeste, il la prémunira par le secours officieux de l'argile durcie: . . . il la distinguera par ce goût qui plaît même dans les villes, quand il assujettit les plus simples fabriques à la pureté des lignes.*'

'*Quand il* [the architect] *aura régularisé l'opinion qu'on peut se faire du besoin, il sera à l'abri des modes et des distances que les hommes légers inventent pour autoriser des manies pompeuses qui retardent, pour des siècles, la pureté du goût.'*

'On verra qu'ici le pauvre a ses besoins satisfaits comme le riche; on verra qu'il n'est pauvre que du superflu.'

'Voulez-vous avoir des idées justes? pensez par vous-même. Voulez-vous être grand dans tous les genres? affranchissez-vous des entraves qui gênent l'expression du sentiment dans les arts.'

Ledoux, *L'Architecture*, pp. 5, 105, 106 and 132

To put the matter briefly, Ledoux advocated a functional style which emphasized simplicity and, although based on utilitarian requirements, also expressed moral principles, emotions, and a new social consciousness of the individual character. He has been admired for his novel artistic qualities, and his emphasis on cubic and other stereometric basic forms. But in these fields Boullée preceded him. Ledoux's specific and individual contribution to architectural development lay in his emphasis on social conditions which embraced the workers, labourers and the poor, without further qualifications, and included the sick.

The interdependence of abstract thought and practical requirements, based both directly and indirectly on social conditions, is clearly apparent in the history of architecture, and particularly in the works of the great planners who express a visionary or Utopian element. The social stresses of the pre-Revolutionary period in France favoured change, and gave an impetus to plans rather than to realizations – a situation not without parallel at the present time. When Napoleon took up some of the schemes previously outlined, he adapted them without taking over their most significant aspects: replacing, for example, the development of whole towns or districts by the opening up of avenues, such as the Rue de Rivoli. The Directoire and Empire styles represent the adaptation of vast civic schemes and functional experiments with simplified ornament, to the requirements of a centralized autocratic state, which used Roman reminiscences to glorify the rulers of the day.[34] The integration of architecture and landscape is clearly demonstrated in Vaudoyer's *Prix* designs of 1783, representing a *ménagerie* – a sort of zoo – as well as a community centre, in which the gardens are also subjected to regular planning.

For Boullée and his followers the situation had been different: unlike their predecessors and successors, they were inspired by the simplicity and austerity of the dwellings of the poorer classes. They saw in bare walls and unbroken surfaces a means of aesthetic expression which, although based on cheap and humble habitations, could be adapted to palaces and civic centres. They reversed, in fact, the more usual situation, in which the rich and aristocratic give the lead to the poor.[35]

Ledoux, unlike Boullée, was in favour of decentralization,

Vaudoyer, Design for a *Ménagerie*; this obtained 1st prize in 1783.

Ledoux, *L'Architecture*, note on p. 215

and in this field he thought England was an example to be emulated. With regard to hospitals he writes: '*Si on ne rougit pas du malheur, on rougit de l'inertie. Au premier coup d'œil les hôpitaux offrent un grand bien; l'Angleterre les a multipliés; la France les a trop concentrés.*'[36]

The dedication of Ledoux's book to Alexander of Russia, *Alexander of the North*, clearly indicates that the aged architect was no Revolutionary, a fact which is apparent throughout his life, since he was imprisoned during the Revolution. He was a Reformist and a radical, who believed in the political promise of the young Czar, a promise which later proved abortive, but which fired the imagination of the ageing and disillusioned man, who had become a writer in order to express his ideas and grievances. How different from this was Boullée's serene detachment in formulating his thoughts with little regard for self-aggrandisement or ambition.

The great contribution of these two contemporary and to some degree complementary personalities, was of significance not only for France, but for European evolution in general. In this connection, it is interesting to note how Italian influence had receded in 18th-century France: Lodoli's ideas, and those

of the *Rigoristi*, who challenged the academic orders in architecture, were unknown (outside the circle of Laugier and his
followers), and even their similarities to Boullée and Ledoux
are more apparent than real, since they are functionalists in a
different sense of the term. The former wanted to expose
structural function as a reaction against the Rococo, and
therefore eschew unnecessary ornament; the latter were guided
by social necessities, which leave their imprint on form.[37]

To sum up: neither Boullée nor Ledoux was a political
revolutionary. In spite of their conservative personal inclina-
tions, they expressed the coming popular taste in architectural
symbols, which became prevalent during the Revolutionary
period and persisted even under the Napoleonic régime. Boullée
and Ledoux show conclusively how an artist's sensitivity can
transcend his conscious views or prejudices and respond to the
social challenge of the time.

A word should be added about Revolutionary decorations,
which replaced the religious processions or ceremonial occasions
of earlier days and acclimatized Neo-Classicism in a popular
and quasi-religious idiom. Here the influence of Jacques-Louis
David's Classicism is quite apparent.[38] Typical are the sculptures connected with the Festival of Unity and Indivisibility of
1793.[39]

French Neo-Classicism Abroad

The influence of French Neo-Classicism in Europe is just as
marked and profound as the French Rococo influence had been
in interior decoration in the early 18th century. Only a few of
the examples which testify to French influence abroad are
mentioned, but they should suffice to illustrate its scope. These
influences are not only important from an art historian's point
of view, but because they express a state of mind, an awareness
of civic ideals and communal attitudes which were regarded as
valuable and worth copying. On the other hand, rural development was neglected and here the English attitude proved more
effective.

The radius of French influence, as distinct from that of the
court of Versailles, spread during this period; it was logical that
the latter, an example of absolute, and from the point of view
of the Enlightenment, reactionary kingship, should lose in
importance as a model. Books of designs, rather than actual
buildings, gained in significance at a time when many grandiose
projects had, by their very nature, to remain unrealized. In this
connection, it would be of great interest to know more of the
competition for the plans for St Petersburg, commissioned by
Catherine the Great in 1764.[40]

Patte, *Monumens*, p. 221

Catherine's activities in the field of architecture were not isolated. They were originally influenced by the French pattern of society, since French ladies of the nobility, whether of ancient families or newly created nobility, acted as patrons in individual cases and on a smaller scale. But as a town-planner she transcended this feminine background and showed herself to be a ruler, just as much as, or more than, any contemporary king.

Although educated women had a place in Renaissance civilization, little building is ascribed to their direct patronage: This situation was drastically altered in 18th-century France, where the great ladies, actresses and mistresses had town and country homes built to their personal requirements. Their

View of Washington, from a 19th-century lithograph.
[See p. 108.]

patronage was considerable, not only in exerting influence, but also from the point of view of quality. Madame de Pompadour was only the outstanding exponent of a general trend. The emphasis on 'sensibilité' (according to the Encyclopédie, under this heading) is characteristic of women and children and is regarded as a powerful physiological and psychological factor; it is reflected in a taste which eschews pomp and evaluates positively the natural and emotional in human intercourse.

A number of buildings executed in Russia are clearly based on Ledoux and the series of Projets for Academy prizes. The Admiralty building in St Petersburg by Zaharov shows an intimate relationship to a Boullée model, since Atlas figures carrying globes flank a side entrance, as in the latter's Royal Library, whilst Thomas de Thomon's Bourse in St Petersburg reflects Ledoux's published architectural designs.[41]

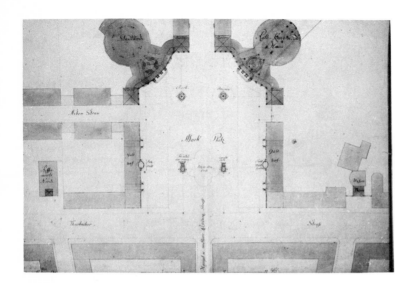

Pedetti, Project of 1788 for the Market-place in Karlsruhe. (By courtesy of the Generallandesarchiv)

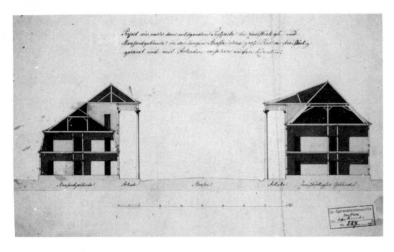

Weinbrenner, Project for the Lange Strasse, Karlsruhe (section). (By courtesy of the Generallandesarchiv)

The influence of Patte's projection of sites for King Louis XV's statue on one master plan undoubtedly inspired Major L'Enfant's conception for Washington, where circuses are superimposed on a grid, thus ensuring variety within regularity in a park-like landscape. Particularly subtle is the relation between the White House and the Capitol, which are connected by a subsidiary axis rather than a main one.[42] These plans, executed in 1791, had in turn their repercussions in France, where they were exhibited after 1793.[43]

Germany was particularly important as a focus for French influences, not only for aesthetic, but also for political and cultural reasons, since the multitude of small states vied with each other in their artistic achievements. Maurizio Pedetti, although an Italian, was profoundly influenced by French

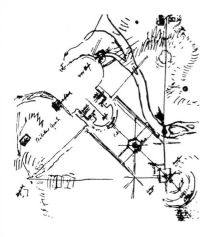

Gilly, Sketch for a Sea-port. After Rietdorf.

taste. He was the architect of the court of Eichstätt, and was also concerned with the plans of 1788 for the market-place in Karlsruhe.[44]

The most outstanding personality was perhaps Friedrich Gilly (1771–1800), whose plan for an ideal city is certainly indebted to French ideas on town-planning, and appears to have been based originally on Patte's multifocal prototypes. French influence was also apparent in the projects for the monument to King Frederick II of Prussia in Berlin, of which a whole series exists, Gilly's being the most important (between 1787 and 1797). Unfortunately, all these plans proved abortive.[45]

Gilly's simple, austere and monumental forms are indebted to Boullée, and the same may be said of the pyramid dedicated to the memory of the Margrave Carl Wilhelm by Weinbrenner (1768–1826) in Karlsruhe in 1823.[46] Here the relationship was based on the intermediary of the *Projets*, which enjoyed European popularity. Weinbrenner's emphasis on multifocal planning in his designs for the connected squares in Karlsruhe between 1801 and 1810, also shows French influence, as does the projected arrangement of giant colonnades for the Lange Strasse of 1808, changing two-storeyed buildings into three-storeyed ones.

Weinbrenner's fan-like plan incorporated religious as well as secular buildings, including both Protestant and Catholic churches, and a synagogue. In the spirit of Ledoux, the city is set in a landscape, while subsidiary architectural centres contrast with the regularity of the main design.

In earlier periods Italian influence had spread throughout Europe; then in the early 19th century, the French impact was felt on Italy. This is shown by a happy find of a number of Boullée's drawings in the Print Room of the Uffizi in Florence, which seem to form part of the illustrations of his *Architecture, Essai sur l'art*, and supplement those of the Print Room of the

Weinbrenner, Project for the Lange
Strasse, Karlsruhe (view). (By courtesy
of the Generallandesarchiv)

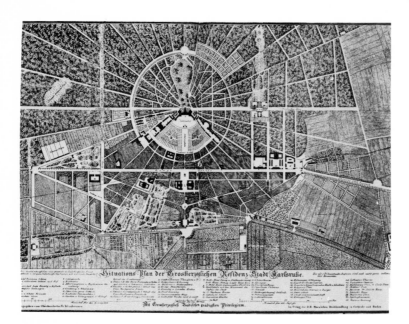

Weinbrenner, Engraving of 1822 showing a Comprehensive Plan for Karlsruhe.

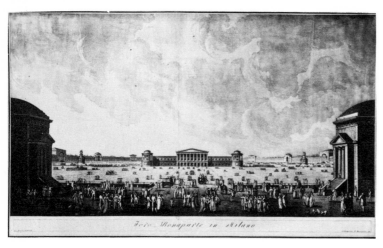

Antolini, View of the projected Foro
Bonaparte, Milan.

Antolini, Ground-plan of the projected
Foro Bonaparte in Milan.

Bibliothèque Nationale. They have not been put to any
practical use, although they appear to have reached the
Library at an early date. Another of Boullée's drawings, signed
and marked '*invenit*', and dated 1782, belongs to the Royal
Institute of British Architects.[47] These two important examples
show that the influence of Boullée's work penetrated further
than has hitherto been suggested, and was not only followed by
his countrymen and practising architects, but was also appreciated by connoisseurs abroad.

The French influence may be partly accounted for by the
prestige of Napoleon, but Canova certainly played an important
part as well. Canova, the friend of Giovanni Antonio Selva, may

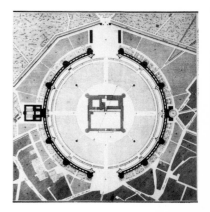

have acquainted the latter with Vaudoyer's publications. At any rate, as Professor Pevsner pointed out, a design for a pyramid with a portico-like Doric entrance was intended by Selva for a monument to Napoleon, to be erected on Mont Cenis.[48] Characteristically, these designs were not executed: their austere monumentality was alien to Italy, and clashed with the architectural tradition of the country. But the Mausoleum of Canova in Possagno, designed by Selva, and the layout of Giuseppe Valadier's Piazza del Popolo and Pincio in Rome are outstanding examples of the acceptance in Italy of alien French taste.[49] Even more arresting are Giovanni Antonio Antolini's plans for a huge square, the Foro Bonaparte in Milan, including a *chemin de ronde* encircling the restored Castello Sforza.[50]

---

1. E. Cassirer, *The Philosophy of the Enlightenment*, Princeton University Press, 1951.

2. Lavedan II, p. 211 ff.

3. A monograph on Patte would be desirable. cf., however, the assessment by W. Hegemann and E. Peets, *The American Vitruvius*, Architectural Books, 1922, *passim*.

4. *Voltaire: Œuvres complètes*, Vol. XXIII, Paris 1879, p. 297 ff.

5. Patte, *Mémoires*, Paris 1769, *passim*.

6. L. Réau, *J.-B. Pigalle*, Paris 1950, p. 51 ff. Also S. Rocheblave, *J.-B. Pigalle*, Paris 1919, p. 57 ff.

7. On Diderot's artistic theories concerning painting which can be regarded as the forerunners of these attitudes, cf. W. Folkierski, *Entre le classicisme et le romantisme*, Paris 1925, *passim*. cf. also the edition of Diderot's *Salons* by J. Seznec and Jean Adhémar, Oxford 1957. Incidentally, Boullée's opinion, detrimental to St Peter's in Rome, is based on the part written by Montesquieu of the article on '*goût*' in the *Encyclopédie*. The latter, however, stresses the element of surprise, based on size, and compares St Peter's to the Pyrenees, a positive evaluation in the direction of the sublime.

8. A special monograph is still needed on the relationship between Lodoli, Cordemoi and Laugier to supplement Kaufmann's studies. cf. W. Herrmann, *Laugier and 18th Century French Theory*, London 1962. cf. also note 16 below.

9. M.-J. Peyre, *Œuvres d'architecture*, Paris 1765.

10. L. Benoist, *Versailles et la monarchie*, Paris 1947, p. 64 ff.

11. Sobry still expressed similar views in his *Poétique des arts*, Paris 1810.

12. cf. W. F. Falls, *Buffon et l'agrandissement du jardin du roi à Paris*, Philadelphia 1953, and M. Morin, *Œuvres de Buffon*, as well as many other editions. A.-N. de Condorcet's treatise, '*L'Esquisse d'un tableau historique des progrès de l'esprit humain*', is available in a new English translation by J. Barraclough in the Library of Ideas, Oxford 1955, under the title, *Sketch for a Historical Picture of the Progress of the Human Mind*.

13. E. Kaufmann, *Architecture in the Age of Reason*, Harvard and Oxford 1956.

14. E. Kaufmann, *Von Ledoux bis Le Corbusier*, Vienna 1933.

15. H. Sedlmayr, *Verlust der Mitte*, Salzburg 1948. In English translation, *Art in Crisis*, London 1957. Sedlmayr's approach is more appropriate to the description of Indian and Chinese temples. These are constructed under the assumption of an underlying correspondence between the structure of the universe and the architectural plan. The Judaeo-Christian emphasis on direction and the importance of human striving for perfection is absent.

16. On architectural theories in Italy, cf. E. Kaufmann, *Architecture in the Age of Reason*, op. cit., especially for a clear exposition of the influence of Lodoli on Milizia and Algarotti, p. 98 ff. The first edition of A. Memmo's treatise on the Lodolian theory, *Elementi d'architettura lodoliana, ossia l'arte del fabbricare con solidità scientifica e con eleganza non capricciosa* – a significant and for us contemporary-sounding title – was published in Rome in 1786, too late to have influenced French theory. But it is interesting how closely the references to functionalism in taste and simplicity of detail correspond. Lodoli's interests were concentrated on structure and decoration, rather than on town-planning. His works are therefore only of marginal significance for the purpose of this study.

17. cf. Boullée, *passim*. A. M. Vogt, *Boullées Newton Denkmal, Sakralbau und Kugelidee*, Basel and Stuttgart 1969. *Social Purpose, passim*.

18. cf. Foreword, note 2.

19. Boullée, p. 13. A. E. Brinckmann's brilliant essay, *Spätwerke grosser Meister*, 1925, should be mentioned in this connection. Also W. Pinder, *Das Problem der Generation*, Berlin 1926.

20. *Social Purpose*, p. 11.

21. Prieur. cf. on the prizewinners the biographical notes in David de Penanrun, Roux and Délaire, *Les Architectes élèves de l'École des Beaux-Arts*, 2nd ed., Paris 1907, especially p. 157 ff. The volume of *Grands Prix* published by L. P. Baltard and A. L. T. Vaudoyer in 1818, should also be consulted.

22. G. Bardet, *Naissance et méconnaissance de l'urbanisme*, Paris 1951.

23. The full and characteristic title of Ledoux's work is *L'Architecture considérée sous le rapport de l'art, des mœurs et de la législation*, Paris 1804, and posthumously 1846. Of modern works, cf. on C.-N. Ledoux, C. Levallet-Haug, Paris-Strasburg 1934, and M. Raval and J.-Ch. Moreux, Paris 1945.

24. N. Pevsner and S. Lang in *Architectural Review*, May 1956, p. 242 ff.

25. *Social Purpose*, pp. 137 and 138.

26. cf. my article in *Gazette des Beaux-Arts*, March 1964, p. 173 ff. See also Larousse, *Grand Dictionnaire universel du 19ᵉ siècle*, for a brief history, and especially R. Dadet, 'Les Débuts du Creuzot', in *La Vie urbaine*, 1963, p. 81 ff.

27. *Projet proposé par le Sieur Poyet, Architecte du roi et de la ville de Paris*, n.d., but about 1790 and before 14 July 1792, as appears from the text, published by Desenne in Paris. *Loi relative à l'établissement d'un monument sur la place de la Bastille, 27 juin 1792. Extraits du registre des arrêts du Comité de Salut Public*, 25th Floréal, year II, and *passim*, especially with regard to country districts, mentioned under the heading '*Architecture civile nationale*' of 28th Floréal, year II. The style is similar to Boullée's: '*Ils s'attacheront particulièrement à donner à chaque espèce de monument le caractère qui lui est propre*'. cf. also Hautecœur V, p. 207 f.

28. On the 'new towns' of the 18th century, see my review of A. Corboz, *Invention de Carouge, 1772–1792, R.I.B.A. Journal*, October 1969, p. 454.

29. G. Walter, *Babeuf*, Paris 1937, p. 188.

30. A. Dayot, *La Révolution Française*, Paris 1905, p. 127. On the fortifications of Paris, cf. D. H. Pinkney, *Napoleon III and the Rebuilding of Paris*, Princeton 1958, pp. 6 f. and 169 f.

31. H. Rosenau, *The Painter J.-L. David*, London 1948.

32. F. H. Dowley in *Art Bulletin*, 1957, p. 259 ff.

33. cf. the present writer in *The Town Planning Review*, XXII, 1951–2, p. 311 ff., and B. Chapman in *The Town Planning Review*, XXIV, 1953–4, p. 177 ff.

34. A representative collection of examples is found in Allais, Détournelle and Vaudoyer, *Projets d'architecture*, Paris 1806. Also *Annales du Musée* of the corresponding years. cf. Hautecœur V, and Lavedan II. A.-M. Peyre, *Projet de bibliothèque dans le local du Luxembourg*, Paris n.d., but approximately 1795, after the Terror.

35. The opposite situation in literature is discussed by H. M. Chadwick, *The Heroic Age*, Cambridge 1912; his conclusions are equally valid for certain phases of the visual arts.

36. On centralization in France, cf. A. de Tocqueville, *L'Ancien Régime et la Révolution*, 1st ed., Paris 1856.

37. cf. A. Memmo, op. cit. M. Petrocchi, *Razionalismo architettonico e razionalismo storiografico*, Rome 1947, *passim*.

38. H. Rosenau, *The Painter J.-L. David*, op. cit. A. Dayot, op. cit.

39. Hautecœur V, p. 123 ff.

40. L. Réau, *L'Art russe*, Paris 1922, pl. I and p. 8 ff., adds little information on this subject. cf. G. H. Hamilton, *The Art and Architecture of Russia*, Pelican History of Art, London 1954, p. 184 ff. and p. 218. Also Réau, op. cit., and A. Voyce, *Russian Architecture*, New York 1948, especially on Leblond's plan of 1717. On Potemkin's town plans, cf. G. Soloveytchik, *Potemkin*, new ed. London 1949, p. 116 ff.

41. Raval and Moreux, op. cit., p. 67 f.

42. W. Reps, *Monumental Washington*, Princeton 1967.

43. L. Réau, *Le Rayonnement de Paris au XVIIIe siècle*, Paris 1946. This shows up the limitation of the influence of Versailles, which spread mainly to the provincial courts and counteracted the role of Paris. Ever since F. Kimball, in *The Creation of Rococo*, Philadelphia 1943, drew attention to Versailles in this connection, the theory of its preponderant influence has been accepted, although amended in points of detail. cf. also F. Kimball in *Architectural Review*, Boston, U.S.A. 1918, p. 41 ff., and Hegemann and Peets, op. cit., p. 285 ff. E. Peets in *Journal of the American Institute of Architects*, 1927, pp. 115 ff., 151 ff. and 187 ff. Also Hautecœur IV. For a pictorial survey, cf. L. Hautecœur, *L'Art sous la Révolution et l'Empire*, Paris 1953 (the numbers of figs. 67 and 68 should be reversed). *Visionary Architects*, ed. D. de Ménil, Houston 1968.

44. cf. H. and K. Arndt in *Beiträge zur Kunstgeschichte, eine Festgabe für H. R. Rosemann*, Munich-Berlin 1960, p. 249 ff.

45. A. Oncken, *Friedrich Gilly*, Berlin 1935, *passim*. A. Rietdorf, *Gilly*, Berlin 1943.

46. A. Fischer, *Karlsruhe*, Munich 1947, *passim*, and K. Ehrenberg, *Baugeschichte von Karlsruhe*, Karlsruhe 1908. A. Valdenaire, *F. Weinbrenner*, Karlsruhe 1919. (I wish to thank Professor Heydenreich and Dr Lehmann Brockhaus for facilities of study at the Zentralinstitut für Kunstgeschichte in Munich and Dr Martin and Dr Fischel for valuable suggestions with regard to the Weinbrenner material in Karlsruhe.) Thieme-Becker includes an excellent article by P. Hirschfeld on Weinbrenner and a short compilation on Pedetti. cf. also A. Valdenaire, *Karlsruhe, die klassisch gebaute Stadt*, Augsburg 1929, and *Dizionario*, op. cit., based on Thieme-Becker.

47. Kindly communicated by Professor K. Lankheit, University of Heidelberg, and Mr John Harris of the Royal Institute of British Architects, respectively. The drawing in London came into the R.I.B.A. with a collection of drawings given by Sir John Drummond Stewart in 1834.

48. N. Pevsner in *Architectural Review*, August 1957, p. 114. The influence is probably based on the well-known publication of *Projets*, since this contains a *Grand Prix* design for a cemetery by Gasse and a second prize design by Guignet, both of 1799, which show the pyramid with added portico in a similar manner.

49. What Kimball, op. cit., says about Germany, and the influence exerted by France, is equally true of Italy in this period. For a brief discussion of that country, cf. Kaufmann, *Architecture in the Age of Reason*, op. cit., p. 75 ff.

50. cf. G. A. Antolini's monumental work, *Opera d'architettura, ossia, Projetto sul foro che doveva esseguirsi in Milano, etc.*, Milan c. 1807, and C. L. V. Meeks, *Italian Architecture, 1750–1914*, Yale University Press, 1966.

II

The English Contribution

It is one of the paradoxes of history that the Industrial Revolution took place first in England, rather than in France. France, which was highly centralized with political and economic emphasis on the large towns, especially the capital, Paris, seemed, in spite of the Physiocrats, predestined to have a decisive influence on future urban developments; but the very opposite occurred.

England, with its country seats, its squires and merchants living largely on their estates outside the capital, exercised the most powerful influence on architectural practice in the 19th century. But, although industrialization was achieved in England in a relatively short time, the professed ideals of the governing classes remained rural. Some many-storeyed houses were built for workers and apprenticed children, but cottages, semi-detached or terraced, remained the labourers' dwellings in the majority of cases, leading later to the creation of slums where there was an agglomeration of shoddily built houses of the single-storey type. True, these cottages were cheap, but they also continued significantly a dominant aesthetic tradition. On the other hand, factories came to look like mansions, apart from the clock reminding the workers of punctuality and good time-keeping.[1]

A reciprocal movement took place between France and England. Under the influence of Puritanism, England had previously adapted Dutch prototypes of sacred and domestic buildings. Architecture was simple and austere, with few ornamental trimmings, and paved the way for the Palladianism of Lord Burlington and the restrained decorations of the period of the Brothers Adam.[2] This in turn made possible the influence of French artists of the so-called Neo-Classical school, in particular the followers of Ledoux. This group is, however, more aptly described as that of the Classical Reformers.

The French reaction against the Rococo was partly due to English inspiration, leading to a cult of nature and a renewed interest in simplicity, as opposed to ostentation and frivolity. The English notion of the Picturesque had an obvious part to play in this evolution, an element associated with the Sublime, as propounded by Lord Shaftesbury.[3] But it is a gross over-

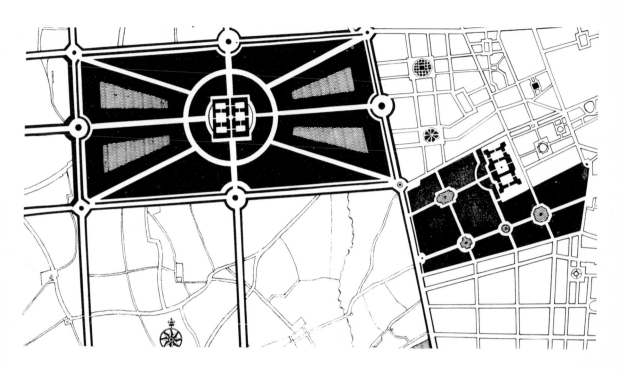

Project for a Royal Palace in Kensington
Gardens, London; after Gwynn's *London
and Westminster Improved.*

simplification to forget the underlying architectural tradition
of sobriety and restraint, which contrasted the landscaped
'English Garden' with a symmetrical and regular Palladian
mansion, thus achieving a synthesis between 'nature' and a
clearly formulated cultural tradition, in which the Picturesque
acted as a stimulus, rather than as the main accent.

The desire for public planning represented a constant
challenge to architects, which was met by Sir Christopher
Wren and Evelyn, among others, with their abortive plans for
London after the Great Fire of 1666. These plans contain
typical examples of the Roman layout of Vitruvian sectors.[4]
John Gwynn, the architect and writer, whose *London and
Westminster Improved* was published in 1766, made an equally
important English contribution.[5] Whilst in Wren's design the
Roman tradition of the Baroque predominates, Gwynn's
regular and symmetrical layout, especially with regard to the
royal palaces and gardens, clearly shows Le Nôtre's influence.
Particularly interesting in this respect is the plan of a square
palace within a circus, connecting Kensington Gardens and
Hyde Park.

Gwynn wished to destroy Westminster Hall completely, as
the ancient roof failed to arouse his admiration, and he also
suggested replacing St James's Palace with one in better taste.
But it would be wrong to dismiss his ideas lightly because those
of our own period have changed. With regard to 'manufactury'
in Birmingham, he was convinced of the importance of

qualitative standards, and envisaged a future for the arts in England by raising the general level of taste for all classes of society. In his broad approach he was thus in the vanguard of his time.

It cannot be denied that English architects, as much as the French, wished to build according to comprehensive plans; Robert and James Adam indicate this quite clearly in the Introduction to their published works. In their opinion it was the lack of public patronage, for which the individual landowner was not a substitute, which inhibited developments on a grand scale:

'Yet we must not expect that the fine arts will ever meet with their most ample reward, or attain their utmost degree of perfection, deprived as they are of that emulation which is excited by public works, and by the honourable applause of a refined and discerning Public.'[6]

Accordingly, the numerous designs by the Brothers Adam in the Sir John Soane's Museum show ambitious layouts for the Houses of Parliament, the Adelphi and other public buildings, but their vision was concentrated on partial solutions and problems, reminiscent of the Baroque.

The additive element is seen particularly clearly in the execution of the sequence of London squares, pleasing in their simplicity, but without dominant accents as far as the city as a unit is concerned.

It is to George Dance the Younger, the Architect and Surveyor to the City of London, that we owe a comprehensive scheme, the development of the crescents and warehouses adjacent to the twin drawbridges for London Bridge. Numerous drawings exist, the first dated 1796; in their fully developed form they include houses with balconies in the crescents on opposite sides of the river, warehouses built on arcades to allow the passage of ships, reminiscent of contemporary pilotis, and terraces upon arches for carts, built on the waterways and docks.[7] The best reproductions of the scheme are found in the *Third Report from the Committee upon the Improvement of the Port of London* of 1800 and an oil-painting, dated 1800, which was bequeathed to the London Guildhall in 1948 by Miss M. S. Dance, one of the last surviving members of the architect's family.[8] Here the interests of trade and aesthetic considerations have been combined in a comprehensive vision, a synthesis of form and function, soon to be broken up by mechanization and historicism. The painting was the model for Daniell's engraving of 1802. Whereas the industrial and domestic buildings are simple and functional in style, the scheme for London Bridge itself was more ingenious than practical: in theory one swing bridge could open for ships, whilst the other, when closed, would allow for the uninterrupted flow of traffic.

Patte's comprehensive plan for Paris, with the symmetrical arrangement of palaces on opposite sides of the Seine, may have inspired Dance's scheme for the development of the 'Legal Quays between London Bridge and the Tower' in 1796. But if it did, the differences are more marked than the similarities. The retention of the Monument shows an understanding of historical values almost absent in Patte, and the simplicity of form contributes a significant and personal element, based on the English tradition.[9]

Like so many of his contemporaries, Dance believed in the significance of architectural tradition and education. From a large sheet in the Sir John Soane's Museum, which includes a survey of his most important works, it seems that he wished to prepare, late in life, a commemorative study which – at least on paper – would seem to suggest the nucleus for a perfect environment. The drawing shows in three rows Ashburnham Palace, the Royal College of Surgeons, Coleorton House, Newgate, Stratton Park, and St Luke's. 'These drawings exhibit the relative dimensions of the buildings delineated being all drawn to the same scale – The Works of George Dance Esq. R.A.' A second drawing, based on the same principle, shows

Left
Daniell, Engraving taken from Dance's painting of London Bridge. Detail.

Left
George Dance the Younger, Project for the London Quays. (By courtesy of the Sir John Soane's Museum, London)

George Dance the Younger, Project for a Banking House in Lombard Street, London – a typical example of his style. (By courtesy of the Sir John Soane's Museum, London)

Newgate Prison and St Luke's Hospital.

The numerous and varied drawings collected in the Sir John Soane's Museum give an indication of the versatility and dignity of the mind of Dance, Sir John Soane's 'revered master'. Soane's idiosyncratic style included projects for numerous monumental schemes, among them the Houses of Parliament. He was successful in his commissions for the Bank of England, the Free Masons' Hall and many others, but he desired further monumental commissions, and a public opinion more alive to architectural values. The rich heritage of his drawings kept in his former house, now the Sir John Soane's Museum, deals with large and representational schemes, but not specifically with London as a whole.[10]

The future, however, belonged to the engineers, rather than the architects. Among them, Thomas Telford was outstanding.

Nash, Plan for Regent's Park.

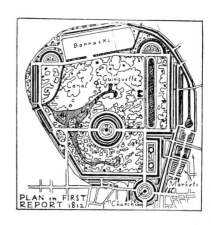

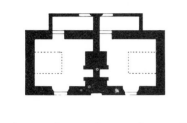

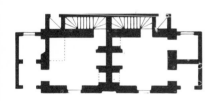

Twin Cottages designed to appear as one, the sham central window creating a *trompe-l'œil* effect; after John Wood the Younger.

He combined technical efficiency with an appreciation of landscape and an interest in Gothic detailing in a Romantic spirit, which gives his work an almost fantastic and haunted look. Some of his projects, such as the one for London Bridge, published in the *Third Report* of 1800 mentioned above, were, like Dance's, unsuccessful, but they nevertheless represent a telling achievement in their combination of technical and artistic qualities. His designs for the Clifton Suspension Bridge reflect a similar spirit. They were superseded by those of Brunel, who adapted the Gothic style to Egyptian forms.[11] Brunel eliminated the two buttress-like supports from the ground, thus increasing the span of the structure. The change illustrates the ever more daring feats of engineering, which slowly replaced the preoccupation with aesthetic matters, a preoccupation which remained of paramount importance to Brunel.

Among English architects, John Nash (1752–1835) was remarkable, especially for his development plan for the area of Regent's Park in London. As first stated in his *First Report of the Commissioners of His Majesty's Woods, Forests and Land Revenues*, of 12 June 1812, this was to include private residences of a luxurious character, barracks, and a zone for three markets.[12] Nash's idea of uniting a large park with housing had already been foreshadowed by Ledoux in his Hosten Estate. Ledoux, in turn, was influenced by the English landscape garden. These facts illustrate the complex cross-currents which obtained between France and England in artistic matters.

The first plan for the park included a circle and two crescents, reminiscent of French planning. Even the name '*guinguette*' for the pavilion is familiar from Ledoux's projects found in his *Architecture*. The theatrical character of many of Nash's façades, of which the triumphal arches leading into mews are a good example, shows the architect's diminishing artistic integrity: a facile brilliance takes the place of the more unobtrusive functional design.

It is understandable that Nash made many enemies, since his far-sighted vision was in advance of his time, and his work was often showy, rather than sensitive. 'Anti-Nashional feeling' existed among the more traditional minds, which was forcibly expressed by the *Anonymous Remarks on the Improvements now in Progress in St. James's Park*, published about 1827.

Even more characteristic of English developments was the contribution of John Wood the Younger in his book *A Series of Plans for Cottages, Habitations of the Labourers, Adapted as well to Towns as to the Country*. It was planned, and the plates executed, in 1781, and a new edition appeared in 1792. Wood's attitude was remarkable, in that he identified himself with the needs of the people to be housed.[13] Of his recommendations, two are particularly illuminating from a sociological point of view:

separate bedrooms should be provided for parents, boys and girls; and cottages should be built in pairs so that the cottagers could be of mutual assistance.

The cottages, containing from one to four rooms, are varied in layout and elevation. They are terraced in a manner which gives them the appearance of a single unit. The windows are supplemented by sham windows which lie along the central axis formed by the partitioning walls, thus giving an impression of unity, although each cottage has a separate entrance.

Continuing the tradition inaugurated by John Wood and strongly influenced in his formal idiom by the French architecture which he saw while travelling to Italy, Joseph Michael Gandy (1771–1843) published two books in 1805, called *Designs for Cottages* and *The Rural Architect*. In the preface to the former he advocated better living conditions for the 'labouring poor', primarily in the country, but also in towns. He published, for example, plans for 'two cones as lodges, thatched to the ground' on an iron framework and a 'Rural Institute' in a sober functional style. His designs for cottages were influenced by John Wood the Younger in their simplicity of form and the introduction of terraced effects. In one of the engravings, the row of cottages forms a closed circle; in another, eight 'satellite' circles, each containing eight rooms, are disposed around a central church or chapel. This latter example is reminiscent of Vaudoyer's design for a '*Ménagerie*', awarded a *Grand Prix* in See p. 105 1783 (*Projets*), which has a similarly rural subject, and consists of a central building surrounded by eight 'satellites'. These alternate between larger circular and smaller square layouts, whereas Gandy preferred uniformity for his surrounding buildings.

Gandy still followed the Palladian tradition, as it was adapted in France, and his emphasis on simplicity shows an affinity to John Wood as well as to Boullée and Ledoux. By sensitive adaptation and original interpretation of form, Gandy thus reveals his true significance in the history of planning. Furthermore, his works combine an imaginative with a functional approach: compared with Gandy's, the picturesque examples of the *Ferme Ornée*, published by John Plaw in 1795 and 1800, are ill-adapted to their purpose.

The impact of the Neo-Classical ideal on the adherents of the Picturesque is clearly illustrated in the title of J. Malton's *An Essay on British Cottage Architecture, being an attempt to perpetuate on principle that peculiar mode of building which was originally the effect of chance*, first published in 1798. Even more interesting is *A Collection of Designs for Rural Retreats as Villas*, of 1802. In both works a systematization of the appearance of the cottage and the old country church is attempted, a systematization which includes Gothic detail, but is nevertheless based on French ideas.

It is applied to 'well chosen irregularity', a basic tenet of the Picturesque. How strongly French influence prevailed is seen in R. Elsam's *Essay on Rural Architecture* of 1803, which attacks Malton, and shows the influence of the *Grand Prix* on a Mausoleum, flanked by pyramids on square bases, and a 'naval pillar', accompanied by two obelisks.

It was this duality which gave vigour to English Romanticism when compared to its German counterpart, for example, where the general climate of opinion fostered a retreat into the individual's confined circle, frequently coupled with a hankering for a non-real medieval world. In France, on the other hand, the Classical tradition remained alive and informed and underlined even totally individualistic and personal utterances during the Romantic movement.

Gandy's painting of '*Architecture, its Natural Model*', discussed by Sir John Summerson,[14] illustrates the French theory of imitation of natural forms, rather than the poetic insight of a Wordsworth. The dichotomy of the period is profoundly expressed by the juxtaposition of this work with the 'Cast-Iron Necropolis', now unfortunately lost, in the Exhibition of the British Academy of 1838. It is certain that Gandy visited France on his way to Italy; also, the series of engravings of the *Grands Prix* and the works of Ledoux were accessible to him among the books of Sir John Soane's private library, so the French influence on his work is based on natural affinity as well as direct knowledge.

Gandy's character is particularly interesting, since he combined a functional approach with a speculative interest in nature studies, and a visionary and dream-like evocation of Antiquity, rendered in numerous drawings, important examples of which are preserved in the Royal Institute of British Architects and the Sir John Soane's Museum. Perhaps it is not altogether irrelevant to recall here the complex psychology of William Blake, and to reflect whether the specific social conditions in England – the combination of a rural background with rapid technological expansion – led to an unusual combination of philanthropic concern with Romanticism. Whilst Romanticism was the expression of an introverted approach, the new demands and problems of the Industrial Age, and the change from village to town life, appear to have fostered an understanding of social relationships and pressures.[15]

Having briefly surveyed the English contribution in the fields of rural and industrial architecture, it seems appropriate to turn to an outstanding achievement in town-planning which left its mark on future developments: the enlargement of the City of Bath.

None of the more famous European cities fully represents the multifocal planning of this period. In Nancy and Bordeaux the development of adjacent piazzas is found, but they are too intimately connected to appear as separate units. The new Edinburgh, although distinguished by many buildings of the highest quality, is, nevertheless, basically a simple linear town, added to the medieval nucleus; the Baroque avenue dominated the structural evolution of Paris; and London remained to a certain extent an agglomeration of villages, as Rasmussen pointed out.[16]

The small city of Bath, however, provides a significant and dynamic example of the synthesis of town and country. Indeed, it is the nearest parallel to Patte's master-plan for Paris, and it is chronologically possible that John Wood the Younger was influenced by it. John Wood the Elder started with Queen Square in 1728, followed by the King's Circus, planned about 1754. The scheme was completed by his gifted son, John Wood the Younger, who erected the Royal Crescent after 1767. (The 'Conveyance in Fee' was paid in 1766.) It is a great achievement: by using a site crowning a hill, the Royal Crescent dominates the city of Bath architecturally, as well as in its elegant detail.[17] The shape of the combined Circus and Crescent achieves an effect of enclosure with variety, and in this sense approximates to Patte's own comprehensive plan of Paris, published in 1765; in this can be seen, among others, Boffrand's design for a market, consisting of adjacent squares and terminating in a large exedra. It should be borne in mind that the competition for the Paris squares took place in 1748, and that the numerous designs connected with it were circulated and discussed before their comprehensive publication by Patte.

The first edition of Laugier's *Essay on Architecture* appeared in English translation in 1755; in this a half-circle, a half-oval, or a half-polygon as the layout for a town entrance is described. On the other hand, the use of sloping hills for gardens had been popular in Italy since the Baroque period. Thus Bath combined French regularity and Italian garden siting with English appreciation of the countryside. Indeed, it is in Bath that the realization of the multifocal city is found, though in an abbreviated form and on a modest scale. Its influence was widespread in England, and can be seen in the planning of many Regency terraces all over the country, especially in the re-development of the Minories and the Camden Town Coliseum Estate, both in London, planned by George Dance the Younger.

From the survey given here it will be seen that an extraordinary complexity characterizes the English scene, in which the rural background and technical developments form the foil for individual achievement. These attain force and consistency with minimal public patronage, whilst the private sector remains the principal force in the rare realization of compre-

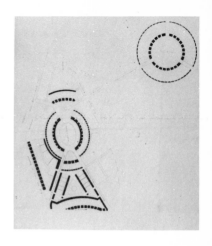

George Dance the Younger, Plan for the Coliseum Estate. (By courtesy of the Sir John Soane's Museum, London)

hensive schemes of town-planning.

English influence abroad was centred on three main aesthetic aspects (of which only a few examples will be given here): the development of landscape gardening; the interest in rural buildings connected with it; and the type of decoration especially popularized in the publications of the Brothers Adam. (The model of Bath proved ineffective outside England.)

The '*style Louis XVI*' is undoubtedly based on English influence, especially in the work of F.-J. Bélanger, who visited England, was on familiar terms with Lord Shelburne and worked in Bowood. Equally, the Abbé Delille had a great admiration for the English garden, although he also appreciated the French style, and refused to choose between the two types: '*Chacun d'eux a ses droits; n'excluons l'un ni l'autre: Je ne décide point entre Kent et Le Nôtre.*' But the most telling example of anglomania in France was perhaps the planning of a new town by the Count d'Artois, which was characteristically to be named

Naysmyth, Designs of 1836 for a New Exchange and Quadrant in Manchester. [See p. 124.]

On Stone & Pr by T. Physick Manchester   J. Naysmyth del. 1836

DESIGNS FOR A NEW EXCHANGE AND QUADRANT,
PROPOSED TO BE ERECTED ON THE SITE OF THE ROYAL HOTEL, FRONTING
Piccadilly, Manchester.

'Nouvelle Londres', but was not carried out.[18]

Sir Benjamin Thompson's (Count Rumford's) projects for a landscaped garden and a soup kitchen in Munich both testify to different aspects of English influence, the aesthetic and the social. The simple façades of regular houses, stressing privacy and a lack of ostentation, characterized George Dance the Younger's work as well as that of his followers. His influence abroad may be gathered from the commission by Sir Benjamin Thompson to supply plans for a 'Thatched Ice House' for his 'English Garden' in Munich in 1791.[19] Of the provincial English cities, Manchester is perhaps not usually associated with ideal planning, but the design by Naysmyth for a new Exchange and Quadrant to be erected there reflects French influence. Liverpool's St George's Hall still provides a dominant accent and core for the expanding township.[20]

When the German architect Schinkel visited England in 1826 he was struck by the façades of private dwellings with a frontage of three to four windows, which in combination had the appearance of 'rows of palaces'. This style, popularized by the Brothers Adam, did not impress the German architect favourably; he did, however, praise the development in technical engineering.[21]

The rural interests characteristic of England were acknowledged by David Gilly in his book *Handbuch der Land-Baukunst* (Berlin 1797–8), when he approvingly quoted John Plaw's works *Rural Architecture* (London 1794) and *Ferme Ornée or Rural Improvements* (London 1795), pointing out that although these cottages are not beautiful, they appear pleasing and well-adapted to their function.

Gilly, *Handbuch*, p. 1

The few suggestions given here attempt to show how, during the period of Enlightenment and of the Industrial Revolution, England was in the forefront of interest in rural buildings and technical achievements, as well as in certain aspects of industrial town-planning, exemplified in George Dance's projects for the comprehensive development of both sides of the river Thames, adjacent to London Bridge. The earlier planning of Bath on a hillside represents not only the adaptation of French and Italian prototypes in an original manner, but also a creation *sui generis*, the influence of which may not even now be exhausted. Furthermore, it should not be forgotten that however irregular or picturesque the English landscaped garden was in its development, the architectural emphasis was on severely classical and symmetrical buildings.

Ideal planning in the abstract was less conspicuous in England than in France; visionary aspects of the city are not lacking, but it is the landscape garden rather than the town which forms the most characteristic and far-reaching contribution to European art.

1. T. S. Ashton, *The Industrial Revolution*, London 1948. *Town Planning Review*, op. cit., Part 2, I, note 26.
2. On the Brothers Adam, cf. *inter alia*, A. T. Bolton, *The Architecture of R. and J. Adam*, London 1922, and J. Lees Milne, *The Age of Adam*, London 1947.
3. Kimball, op. cit., *passim*. Chr. Hussey, *The Picturesque*, London 1927. S. H. Monk, *The Sublime*, New York 1935. N. Pevsner in *Architectural Review*, November 1944, p. 139 ff. J. Stern, *A l'ombre de Sophie Arnould, F.-J. Bélanger*, Paris 1930, *passim*. Hautecœur IV, *passim*.
4. W. G. Bell in *Journal of the R.I.B.A.*, 1918, p. 145 ff.
5. J. Summerson, *Georgian London*, London 1945.
6. Robert and James Adam, *The Works in Architecture* in English and French, London 1773–1822; Preface to Book I, 1776.
7. H. Rosenau on 'Dance' in *Journal of the R.I.B.A.*, 1947, p. 502 ff. J. Summerson, *Sir John Soane*, London 1952. D. Stroud, *G. Dance, Architect 1741–1825*, London 1971.
8. I owe this information to the kindness of the Authorities of the Guildhall Art Gallery, London.
9. Hegeman and Peets, op. cit., p. 84.
10. cf. notes 5 and 7 above.
11. Th. Telford, *Catalogue to the Exhibition at the Institution of Civil Engineers*, London 1957. L. Meynell, *Th. Telford*, London 1957. L. T. C. Rolt, *I. K. Brunel*, London 1957, p. 56 and *passim* and *Th. Telford*, London 1958. F. D. Klingender *Art and the Industrial Revolution*, London 1947, *passim*.
12. J. Summerson, *John Nash*, 2nd ed., London 1949–50. The most important source for the development of a 'Plan of an Estate belonging to the Crown called Marybone Park Farm' is the second plan of the *First Report of the Commissioners of His Majesty's Woods, Forests and Land Revenues* of 12 June 1812.
13. *Social Purpose*, p. 19.
14. On Gandy's suggested political affiliations, about which one would wish to know more, cf. J. Summerson in *Architectural Review*, May 1941, p. 89. Also in *The Architect and Building News*, 1936, p. 38 ff., and in *Heavenly Mansions*, London 1949, pp. 111 ff. and 132 ff. The present writer in *Town-Planning Review*, XXII, op. cit., p. 317 ff.
15. Klingender, op. cit.
16. S. E. Rasmussen, *London, The Unique City*, London 1937.
17. W. Ison, *The Georgian Buildings of Bath*, London 1948. Also Summerson, *Heavenly Mansions*, op. cit., p. 87 ff.
18. Stern, op. cit., I, pp. 4 f., and 97 f. Hamilton, op. cit., *passim*.
19. On Rumford, cf. E. Larsen, *An American in Europe. The Life of B. Thompson, Count Rumford*, London 1953. Rosenau, 'Dance', op. cit.
20. *244, Journal of the University of Manchester Architectural and Planning Society*, No. 5, p. 4 ff. J. Q. Hughes, *Liverpool*, London 1969.
21. L. Ettlinger in *Architectural Review*, May 1945, p. 131 ff.

Part Three

I

Neo-Classicism and Romanticism

It may at first seem surprising to find A.-C. Quatremère de Quincy included in a survey of those architects and Utopian thinkers who were primarily concerned with the vision of ideal cities. Although he did not belong to either of these categories, his position as an art critic and scholar, enhanced by the post of Permanent Secretary of the Paris Academy which he held for many years, influenced the planning of Paris, and made his views known in France and all over Europe; numerous examples of their impact can be traced in artistic fields. He became an arbiter of taste through his writings, especially the funerary orations he delivered to the Academy. In this sense he can be regarded as the Diderot of the 19th century, but, whereas the *Salons* served the present as well as the future, Quatremère's main work consisted in explaining and summing up the past in order to deduce timeless rules. Goethe, for example, valued highly his ideas on the restoration of the Jupiter of Olympia.[1]

In architecture, Quatremère favoured clear and structurally conceived forms, implying a type of town-planning in which uninterrupted vistas dominated, and where individual buildings were singled out for special attention. These principles were applied in Paris to the siting of the Church of the Madeleine at the end of the Rue Royale, and the planned continuation of the Champs-Élysées, which were to be dominated by the Arc de Triomphe. Even Haussmann's boulevards are not entirely unconnected with the Neo-Classical tradition, in their emphasis on the clear-cut *percées* of streets.[2]

The great significance which Quatremère attributed to town-planning can be gauged from the article '*Ville*' in his volume on Architecture in the *Encyclopédie méthodique*, published from 1788 to 1825, especially when compared with the short entry in Diderot's and D'Alembert's *Encyclopédie*. He was aware of the importance of the elevation, as contrasted to the more usual emphasis on the plan; he showed concern for the width of the streets; and he appeared torn between a desire for planning and the '*liberté de se loger*' which he, a liberal-minded thinker, could not help advocating. In spite of this, he voiced misgivings about the appearance of Paris, which in his view was marred by the practice of the aristocracy of hiding their mansions at the bottom of private forecourts.[3]

Quand on se forme une juste idée de cet art [architecture], *et qu'on envisage toute l'étendue des propriétés qu'il embrasse, on voit d'abord qu'étant, avant tout, principe d'ordre . . . c'est de lui que . . . la bonne police et l'administration des villes empruntent leurs dispositions et leurs plus sages règlemens.*

Article 'Ville', Encyclopédie méthodique

According to this primacy of architecture, he upholds the teaching on 'bienséance' and especially on 'convenance' against 'commodité', as already expressed by J.-F. Blondel in his *Cours d'architecture* and in the *Encyclopédie* of Diderot, who says that 'la convenance doit être regardée comme le premier principe de l'art de bâtir'. Quatremère appreciated fitness of style and a sense of formal values, which certainly would have led him to deprecate the present-day obsession with standards of living. His interest in history gave him an understanding of the varied origins of towns, and he was aware that local conditions varied. '*Nous voyons que, presque partout, les villes . . . durent leur origine, à ce qu'on peut appeler les causes fortuites.*'[4]

Quatremère's longevity (1755–1849) obscures the fact that he was a contemporary of Boullée and Ledoux, of Canova and Thorwaldsen, of David and his followers. The theory of Classicism found an intelligent advocate in him; but this age passed when mechanization became a determinant factor. At the time of his death he was tired of people and their opinions: '*J'ai le droit d'être mort*',[5] he replied when refusing an invitation for a social occasion. His personal tastes were unconventional, but he seemed to fight shy of his own conclusions as when, after describing the basic aesthetic principles of Egyptian art as early as 1785, and recognizing its monumentality and durability, he still accorded preference to Greek art.[6]

In his view the function of art was imitation, meaning by the term not an indebtedness to, nor a copy of natural forms, but the exposure of their inherent principles. In this sense, architecture for him was an imitative art. He recognized the limitations of a purely aesthetic approach and the narrowness of the mere connoisseur, and demanded far-ranging intelligibility and thus communication in the arts, as well as the expression of moral principles. For these reasons he deplored formalism for its own sake, and established a theory equally remote from the Rococo or Romanticism. The regulative principle of nature imitating itself is a dialectic, almost Hegelian concept: '*C'est la Nature entière qui devient le type de son imitation.*' We are far removed here from the exuberant and uncritical nature-worship of a Boullée.

Article 'Architecture', Encyclopédie méthodique.

In contrast to the town is a single unit, the *cabane* or hut, which exemplifies for Quatremère the structural principles of

Design for a Primitive Hut; from Perrault's *Vitruvius* (1st ed., 1673). [See p. 132.]

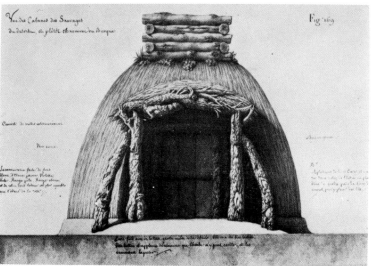

Lequeu, Design for a Primitive Hut. (By courtesy of the Bibliothèque Nationale, Paris) [See p. 132.]

support and weight, as well as the synthesis between beauty and function. Here he differs from Vitruvius and his followers, among them Perrault, Laugier, Chambers, Milizia and to a certain extent Lequeu, for whom the empirical primitive hut was the basis of imitation. The Vitruvian illustrations by Jean Goujon for Martin include the hut; and the intended architectural publication by Lequeu contains a drawing of a '*Vue des Cabanes des Sauvages du désert, et, plutôt chaumine des Basques*'. The concept of the 'noble savage' is superimposed on the Vitruvian tradition.[7]

Article '*Architecture*', *Encyclopédie méthodique*.

In his treatise, *Considérations morales sur la destination des ouvrages de l'art*, published in Paris in 1815, Quatremère combines an interest in the function of the work of art with a pronounced antipathy for a solely utilitarian or, as he calls it, materialistic approach; in his view, unmitigated utility threatens the arts. Art is in fact not the same as industry, and mechanization is regarded as unfavourable to artistic creation. The enlightened patron, who can distinguish the spiritual approach, is called for, a patron who rejects vulgar subject matter. '*Le goût du luxe tient au principe sensuel, le goût du beau au principe moral.*' Whilst moral art is lasting, the purely fashionable and sensual is ephemeral. '*Généralement, tout ouvrage dénué de la perspective d'un emploi moralement utile ne saurait procurer à l'âme de l'artiste, ou du spectateur, cette passion qui exalte le talent de l'un et l'admiration de l'autre.*' This clearly shows the almost Puritan element which underlies so much of Neo-Classical artistic theory.

Quatremère de Quincy, *Considérations*, p. 15

Considérations, p. 25

For Quatremère the relation between the arts and morals was evident. The social function of the former demanded not only that they should uplift, instruct and truly educate, but also that they should be generally understood and easily accessible. For these reasons he opposed the Napoleonic spoliations of Italian art treasures, but raised no objection to the Elgin Marbles finding their way to the British Museum, which was free and open to all. However, he disliked museums in general, and the Gothic style in particular. This made him the enemy of Auguste Lenoir and the Musée de l'Art Français, which was primarily intended to illustrate the past of France.[8] His historical interests led him not only to archaeological research on the tomb of Porsenna, the reconstruction of the Zeus of Olympia and other specialist studies, but also to a survey of the buildings of Paris, which forms the second part of the first volume of J. G. Legrand's and C. P. Landon's *Description de Paris* of 1806–9. Here Quatremère gives many hints as to the siting of public buildings, always emphasizing structural principles and the significance of the function of ornament. This central position between the ideal and the practical and sensual places him in line with the Classicist theory of art, as outlined by Bellori, and re-assessed fairly recently in

Panofsky's *Idea*.[9] But there is a significant difference, since, for Quatremère, moral teaching and the use and principles of structure replace the emphasis on the contrast between realism and idealism.

Because of the novelty of his terms of reference and their application to architectural and planning developments, Quatremère's theoretical and historical writings are still revealing today: he discussed and criticized, for example, the small-minded decorations and the red-coloured marble against white stone of the Arch of the Tuileries, and deplored the changed use of the Hôtel de Salme, designed originally by P. Rousseau and turned into a palace for the Légion d'Honneur. The lowering of standards due to a neglect of function is pithily expressed in the statement: *'toute maison prétend à être un palais et tout palais affecte l'air d'un lieu public'*.

Quatremère de Quincy's book on his friend Canova not only expresses his admiration for the artist, but is also perhaps the fullest survey of the theory of Neo-Classicism in its aims of archaeological correctness and formal consistency.[10] He emphasizes novelty of subject matter as a positive factor, as when, for instance, Pauline Borghese, Napoleon's sister, is represented as Venus Victrix, or Laetitia Ramolini, his mother, is modelled on Agrippina. According to Quatremère, the creative achievement here is by no means inferior to that of the Ancients, especially as the addition of spiritual grace is without precedent in the past. He thus demanded an open-minded approach towards new developments, and emphasized the meaning of the subject, and the function of the work.[11]

Having attempted to survey the basic tenets of Quatremère de Quincy, it now remains to clarify his place in the Neo-Classical movement, and the development of its attitudes. Basically, the view of life at this period was optimistic. Jacques-Louis David may be considered an outstanding exponent of Neo-Classicism, and it will be seen that he was convinced of the influence of art on life; in other words, although archaeological correctness was sought, it was not an aim in itself. The aim was rather to resuscitate the Roman virtues with the Roman style. This is why the Etruscan order found great favour, as it was meant to stand for noble simplicity and virtue; the same appears true of architectural works: the Classical ideal was to serve life.

Percier and Fontaine, both pupils of A.-F. Peyre, were acquainted personally with Quatremère and shared many of his views. Their contribution to the rebuilding of Paris represents only part of the latter's aspirations,[12] since their planning was piecemeal and they laid stress on rich ornaments unconnected with function. In the collaboration of Percier and Fontaine, the former was more a designer and the latter an engineer. The period of mechanization is significant not so

Legrand and Landon, *Description*, Vol. II, p. 90

much for the devaluation of symbols, as Giedion suggests, but
for their elimination, the engineer and the decorator taking the
place of the artist. This led to the primacy of the functional
approach to architecture, which was regarded as far superior
to the merely ornamental and decorative. Solutions of aesthetic
quality were obtained in the cases of bridges and railway
stations.[13]

It was during this period that competition for the planning of
towns reached perhaps its fullest expansion. The Neo-Classical
development of Munich led practically to a 'new town', and
the same can be said of Georgian Edinburgh. Although these
plans were realized, and did not claim to express any absolute
or universal values, they were nevertheless influenced by such
tenets, and derived their comprehensiveness and spaciousness
from a disregard of narrowly utilitarian considerations. Plans
for buildings designed to serve a multiplicity of purposes are
characteristic of the period.

The Panopticon by Samuel Bentham, which could be used
as a school, a prison, or a workhouse, is perhaps the best-known
example of this type of structure. Derived from the Mannerist
ideal town in outline, it has a novel social purpose: it is a house
which is in itself a small city – a concept foreshadowed by
Alberti. Its reformative character is typical of the period, during
which many designs for prisons were produced which showed a
characteristic concern for moral and hygienic reform, rather
than any desire to add to punishment.[14]

The foregoing pages give an indication of the complexity
of an age in which Neo-Classicism, based on archaeological
accuracy, was confronted with a new and frankly moralizing
approach. The explanation suggested by Zeitler[15] in his interesting study *Klassizismus und Utopia*, gives a partial solution to the problem, since he concentrates on the dualistic
or Utopian nature of the Neo-Classical period; it seems,
however, that his is an over-simplification. The term Utopian
itself is by definition dualistic, since it presupposes a non-
existent and impossible social order. Utopia, Revolution or
Reform – these three possibilities of change – are all found
about 1800, however, and one could hardly say that Goethe's
views supported the aesthetics of, say, a Canova, or the political
leanings of a David.

Goethe warned that his Pedagogical Province of *Wilhelm
Meister's Travels* should not be regarded as a Utopia, since the
possible and the impossible can be realized in images. In the
words of Goethe's Leonardo:

*Unser alter Freund . . . erzählte . . . mir gar manches von einer päda-
gogischen Verbindung, die ich nur für eine Art von Utopian halten
konnte; . . . Weil ich ihn aber kenne, weil er gern durch Bilder das*

Wilhelm Meister, Book I, 11

Mögliche und Unmögliche verwirklichen mag, so liess ich es gut sein, und nun kommt es uns zu Gute; er weiss gewiss Ihnen Ort und Umstände zu bezeichnen.

The city of the Pedagogical Province is described in detail. The streets afford a wide diversity of views, the buildings reveal their function by their exterior, whilst the suburbs, skirted by fields, are followed by garden dwellings.

Den . . . Wanderer musste nunmehr in Verwunderung setzen, dass die Stadt sich immer zu erweitern, Strasse aus Strasse sich zu entwickeln schien, mannigfaltige Ansichten gewährend. Das Aussere der Gebäude sprach ihre Bestimmung unzweideutig aus, sie waren würdig und stattlich, weniger prächtig als schön. Den edlern und ernsteren in Mitte der Stadt schlossen sich die heitern gefällig an, bis zuletzt zierliche Vorstädte anmutigen Stils gegen das Feld sich hinzogen, und endlich als Gartenwohnungen zerstreuten.

Wilhelm Meister, Book II, 8

This description evokes not only the French taste of the time and its stress on functionalism, but also emphasizes the growth of the garden suburb, then seen as a positive factor in planning. The shortcomings of the sprawling city were still unknown.

The combination of aesthetic and social considerations which had prompted the impact of Neo-Classical architecture on town-planning led to the rebuilding of important sections of many European cities, among which Munich is outstanding.[16] One of the most interesting architects of the period was Carl von Fischer (1782–1820), whose short and brilliant career in Munich led to the erection of several buildings in commanding positions, such as the Prinz-Karl-Palais, combining the reconciliation of the French tradition of detailing with an Italian emphasis on dramatic vistas.[17]

The plans for the development of the external area of Munich, bordered by the Karls-Tor, one of the medieval

Carl von Fischer, Design of 1810 for the Karls-Tor, Munich. (By courtesy of the Stadtarchiv)

western city gates rebuilt in 1861, were laid under his influence, and his design (1810) for the reconstruction of the gate itself shows an individual treatment of the orders, set against a rusticated basement storey, with additional symbolic sculpture in the French tradition.

Another important artist of international reputation in Munich was Andreas Gärtner (1744–1826), who travelled widely to Vienna, Berlin and Paris, and settled for some time in Paris in about 1780 as an architectural inspector. His drawing for a centralized building in a garden, executed in Paris in 1778, shows the marked influence of the *Grands Prix* and all they stand for in clarity and precision, and demonstrates their European significance.

It is against this background that the competition of 1808 for the replanning of the Karolinenplatz and Königsplatz in Munich has to be seen. Stengel, Sckell (mainly known as a garden designer), Riedl, Rudersheimer and Praendtl each produced one design; Thurn, Gärtner (probably Andreas) and Dietrich two, and Schadl three. These Vitruvian sectors and multifocal layouts have been overshadowed by later developments, but are still worth studying, especially as most are the work of comparatively unknown men. The series of 10 unsigned drawings in the Historisches Stadt-Museum may well be connected with this project. (Material on the architects can be found in the Kreisarchiv, Munich.)

The French impact, to which a certain traditional Baroque heaviness is added, also appears in an anonymous Munich drawing of a '*Templum Pacis*', commemorating the victories of Napoleon in Ulm and Austerlitz about 1805.

Leo von Klenze (1784–1864), famous for his work in Munich, possessed a wide knowledge of the cultural trends of his period. He was well acquainted with the work of Quatremère de Quincy, whom he mentioned approvingly. He also cites Schinkel, whom he considered a great master. His independent mind reassessed traditional values, and adapted them to the

A. Gärtner, Design for Circular Buildings in a Garden Setting. (By courtesy of the Technische Hochschule, Munich)

Anonymous drawing of a *Templum Pacis* in honour of Napoleon's victories at Ulm and Austerlitz. (By courtesy of the Technische Hochschule, Munich)

needs of his own day. When discussing the requirements of the Christian Church[18] in his *Anweisung zur Architectur des christlichen Cultus* of 1834, he advocated the fusion of the Neo-Classical style with the Christian ritual. In his opinion the underlying ideas of the Greek religion were close to the Christian revelation, and for this reason classical forms could be perfectly adapted to the novel purpose of church architecture, though Roman basilicas would be more suitable than the Gothic style. So for him Classicism was not primarily derivative, but creative. He invented a new terminology for the art of the Middle Ages, which he admired in many ways, wishing to have it described as 'hieratic', in order to stress the identity of the social and architectural structures of the period. His most characteristic passages are perhaps those which refer to the importance of history as a means of assessing the present as well as the past. He studied the development of towns as a whole, and demanded a single general idea of city planning. If this was absent, important individual buildings could be created; in this way a 'Villa Hadriana' might be achieved, but no 'Athens and Rome'. Altogether, he was an enemy of eclecticism, demanding reinterpretation and adaptation, and eschewing the mere copying of Greco-Roman models.

The strong influence of French Classicism was not only seen in the formal means employed by Klenze, but went so far as to cause the use of French terms such as '*guinguette*', for a pleasure pavilion in a park, or a '*Monument de la Pacification*', dated between 1813 and 1816. Klenze's contemporary, Friedrich von Gärtner (1792–1847), who had been a pupil of Percier and Fontaine in 1814, was even more directly influenced by France, as shown, for example, in his designs for festival buildings with accompanying columns as torch holders. Gärtner eclipsed Klenze, who was in disfavour with King Ludwig I. As President of the Bavarian Academy, he emphasized the Classical prototypes in a stereotyped manner far removed from the individual interpretations of a Quatremère or a Klenze.

Planning in England during the period of Neo-Classicism appears rather piecemeal when compared with the Age of Enlightenment. The single unit, rather than the comprehensive plan, came to the fore, as perhaps best seen in Robert and Sidney Smirke's British Museum, a traditional form with its temple façade and circular library, associated with and adjacent to older and newer squares.[19] The weakening of the town-planning impulse is perhaps best illustrated by the largely abortive plans for Trafalgar Square. Goldicutt bitterly criticized the decisions of the Committee which decided to erect a column as a Nelson Monument in Trafalgar Square. His own solution had been a square pedestal, supporting a 'terrestrial globe, over which he [Nelson] sailed triumphant'. He complained that among 'the hundred and more designs' the worthless had been chosen; he regretted that no more monumental accent had been selected. Goldicutt was deeply indebted to the French tradition, as represented by the *Projets*, and also because of his personal studies with Leclère in France before 1817. As an alternative to the Nelson column, he had designed a new layout centred on the 'London Amphitheatre', intended as 'a National Building to concentrate the Scientific Bodies of the Metropolis'. The National Gallery, the College of Physicians and Union Club House, as well as St Martin's-in-the-Fields, were to be preserved, and houses so arranged as to form an architectural balance.[20]

These few plans illustrate the fact, already suggested with regard to the Brothers Adam, that numerous architects in England were eager to obtain public commissions to be built in a monumental style, and that they often eschewed the Picturesque and Romantic. It is on this basis that the deep French influence on English art in the late 18th and early 19th centuries rested.[21]

In the less known provincial English towns, attempts at planning may also be noted. For example, interest in developing Manchester as a centre became apparent during the 19th century, as was expressed in William Fairbairn's essays and James Naysmyth's designs for 'improvements', published in 1836. These included a circular Exchange or University, fore-

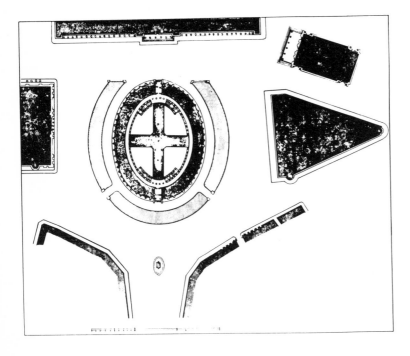

Project for Trafalgar Square, after Goldicutt.

shadowing the present layout of the Central Library and Town Hall, surrounded by a crescent. In Naysmyth's design appears the circular feature of the colonnaded Exchange, in the tradition of French Classicism, popularized in England by Nash's Regent Street and Regent's Park, London, whilst the crescent shows the influence of contemporary planning in Edinburgh, which was familiar to him. This adjoining crescent, or 'Quadrant' as Fairbairn called it, is a plain four-storeyed structure, enhanced by classical orders, the ornamental parts being concentrated on the ends of the wings.[22]

A. W. N. Pugin's *Contrasts*, published in 1836, are interesting from the point of view of the ideal planner, since he expected the renewal of the Catholic religion to lead to a 'revolutionary reaction' in architecture, if this phrase may be allowed. In this basic attitude he is akin to the Neo-Classical thinkers and architects, although his values are reversed and he extols the Middle Ages.[23] Indeed, ever since the *Querelle des Anciens et des Modernes* in the 17th century and before, European artistic evolution had been based on a conflict between the supporters of Antiquity – whether in its Greek or Roman form – and the adherents of the contemporary style. Parallels between the past and present were drawn as late as the beginning of the 19th century. J.-N.-L. Durand's *Recueil et parallèle des édifices de tout genre, anciens et modernes*, published in year IX of the Revolution, is a typical example of the popular series of publications which compared the old and the new. What singles out Pugin in this respect is his wholesale condemnation of the present and his unqualified admiration for the past. On the other hand, in his stress on the relation between art and life, and the religious meaning expressed in church architecture, he is typical of his period. His dogmatic approach is more akin to the intellectual climate obtaining in France than in England, a fact which may, at least in part, be explained by his French origin and his frequent visits to that country.

John Martin (1789–1854) should also be mentioned here, not so much for his unusual designs for a barrel-vaulted monumental arch for Park Crescent, London, of 1820, as for his visionary representation of Satan seated on the hemisphere in 'Satan Presiding at the Infernal Council' of 1824, illustrating, although not exactly, Book II of Milton's *Paradise Lost*. Emphasis on the geometric form may well be based on an adaptation of French prototypes. The earlier vision of the Fall of Babel of 1819, including a square tower of many tiers, seems to have been resuscitated for the contemporary spectator in Dr Charles Holden's Senate House of London University, designed in 1931. The dichotomy between vision and technique is resolved by Martin's interest in the 'drainage of the Metropolis and preservation of sewage', and the siting of railways[24] –

examples of his concern for 'adequate employment' and technical improvement.

    The contrast to these tendencies can perhaps be no better
illustrated than in Sir Jeffrey Wyatville's evocative studies of
medieval castles or his 'Palace of Circe', found in an album of
drawings in the Print Room of the British Museum; the latter
shows a huge gothic-style building emerging from the mist, an
illustration to which the following characteristic verses are
appended:

> From a high point I marked a distant view,
> A stream of curling smoke ascending blue,
> And spiry tops, the tufted trees above,
> Of Circe's palace bosomed in the grove.

The relation between Greek mythology and the Romantic
English landscape setting could not be more intimate.[25]

    Mechanization set in more drastically in architecture and
the crafts than in town-planning. Its impact on the former was
felt in the work of architects from the Napoleonic period to
more recent times. Nevertheless, when studying the evolution of
Neo-Classicism, it becomes apparent that this was far more
positive a force than was conceded by some. The frank acknowledgement of social necessities, the dynamic endeavour to reconcile the day-to-day aims with lasting values, may well still
act as an inspiration, when fully understood. It is perhaps not

John Martin, Mezzotint of 1819 showing
a Vision of the Fall of Babel. (By courtesy
of the British Museum)
[See p. 139.]

without interest that in the fields of literature and philosophy the quality of thought of the Germans – Goethe, Schiller and Kant, to give a few examples only – has been internationally recognized, whilst the visual arts of the period have not, so far, been as widely appreciated.

Neo-Classical art, studied especially by Wölfflin and his followers among art historians, is slowly coming into its own again. In the field of sculpture, Zeitler has made a major contribution. But the consideration of architecture is not, as yet, so far advanced; in particular, the relationship between artistic theory, the ideal master plan, and the architecture of numerous European cities deserves fuller exploration.

This brief survey has attempted to show that the impact of the Neo-Classical theory on town-planning was neither sterile nor fruitless as regards new ideas. The ambivalénce lies not in this theory itself, but in the growing power of mechanization, of which Giedion has so fully and lucidly explored the trends. It is in these contrasting tendencies between two rival and antagonistic attitudes that the specific character of the period is found.

1. H. Jouin, *A.-C. Quatremère de Quincy*, Paris 1892. cf. also R. Schneider, *L'Esthétique classique chez Quatremère de Quincy*, and by the same author, *Quatremère de Quincy et son intervention dans les arts*, both Paris 1910.

2. J. M. and B. Chapman, *The Life and Times of Baron Haussmann*, London 1957.

3. On the problem of Classicism, Romanticism and Utopia, cf. R. Zeitler, *Klassizismus und Utopia*, Stockholm 1954, *Figura V*, especially with regard to Canova. Quatremère, article 'Ville' in *Architecture, Encyclopédie méthodique*, III, p. 598. Incidentally, the second volume of the *Encyclopédie méthodique* was published from 1801 onwards, and not, as Zeitler suggests, in 1820. It differs only slightly from the *Dictionnaire historique d'architecture* of 1832. H. Kiener in *Festschrift H. Wölfflin*, Munich 1924, p. 291 ff. Boullée, p. 19. For a general survey of Classicism, cf. P. Klopfer, *Von Palladio bis Schinkel*, Eszlingen 1911. Useful summaries are found in Rose G. Kingsley, *A History of French Art*, London 1899, *passim*.

4. Article 'Ville' in *Architecture, Encyclopédie méthodique*, III, p. 590 ff.

5. Jouin, op. cit., p. 76.

6. The most important works are *Considérations morales sur la destination des ouvrages de l'art*, Paris 1815, and *Essai sur la nature . . . de l'imitation dans les beaux arts*, Paris 1823 (English translations of both works appeared in 1821 and 1837 respectively); *De l'universalité du beau*, Institut Royal de France, 24 April 1827; *Histoire de la vie et des ouvrages des plus célèbres architectes*, Paris 1830; and *Architecture*, part of the *Encyclopédie méthodique*, Paris 1788–1825.

7. The present writer in *Architectural Review*, August 1949, p. 111 ff. A. W. Herrmann, op. cit., stresses the similarity between Quatremère's and Laugier's concepts of the primitive hut.

8. A. Wittlin, *The Museum*, London 1949, fails to discuss this collection. cf. H. Rosenau, *The Painter J.-L. David*, London 1948, *passim*, and Boullée, p. 15. cf. L. von Klenze and L. Schorn, *Beschreibung der Glyptothek*, Munich 1830, a gallery mainly devoted to antique sculpture.

9. E. Panofsky, *Idea*, Hamburg 1924, *passim*.

10. cf. Zeitler, op. cit., on the 'antithetic' element in Canova's art.

11. Quatremère de Quincy, *Canova*, Paris 1834, pp. 142, 238, 312 f.

12. P. Lafond, *L'Art décoratif et le mobilier sous la République et l'Empire*, Paris 1900. M. Fouché, *Percier et Fontaine*, Paris 1905, *passim*. On the development of Paris. cf. Lavedan II, *passim*; M. Poëte, *Formation et évolution de Paris*, Paris 1910; G. Bardet, *Naissance et méconnaissance de l'urbanisme*, op. cit.

13. S. Giedion, *Mechanisation Takes Command*, Oxford University Press, 1948, p. 328 ff. The same author gives a fuller acknowledgement of Percier and Fontaine as architects in *Space, Time and Architecture*, first published in 1941. On the primacy of decoration and ornament during the Empire, cf. *Recueil des décorations exécutées . . . d'après C. Percier et P. L. F. Fontaine*, Paris 1807, which illustrates the ceremonial connected with Napoleon's coronation. A *Description des cérémonies . . . pour le mariage de S.M. l'Empereur Napoléon avec I.A.S. Madame l'Archiduchesse Marie-Louise*, Paris 1810, shows the designs of the two architects; the engravings are by Normand. No conflict of loyalties between the two Empresses seems to have disturbed them, since they did not set themselves up as moralists. cf. M. Fouché, op. cit. Also Hautecœur V, p. 143 ff.

14. N. A. Hans, *New Trends in Education in the 18th Century*, London 1951. A succinct biography of the two brothers Bentham is found in the *Dictionary of National Biography*; *Social Purpose* passim.

    A telling example of social considerations and the emphasis on improvement is found in L. Baltard, *Architectonographie des prisons*, Paris 1829, which gives a full survey, and criticizes English layouts, whilst praising the *panoptique*; Vaudoyer's *Dissertation sur l'architecture*, dated 1823, a manuscript copy of which is in the Royal Institute of British Architects, clearly shows the influence of Boullée's aesthetic judgement.

15. R. Zeitler, op. cit., *passim*.

16. cf. Klopfer, op. cit., and H. Beenken, *Das neunzehnte Jahrhundert in der deutschen Kunst*, Munich 1944.

17. On C. von Fischer, cf. the unpublished thesis by Dr Schindler.

18. L. von Klenze, *Anweisung zur Architectur des christlichen Cultus*, Munich 1834, especially p. 26 ff. Also H. Kiener in *Thieme-Becker* and his unpublished thesis, Munich 1921. O. Hederer, *Die Ludwigstrasse*, Munich 1942. J. Widenhofer, *Die bauliche Entwicklung Münchens*, Munich 1916. H. Kreisel, *München*, Munich-Berlin 1950.

19. N. Pevsner in *Architectural Review*, March 1953, p. 179 ff.

20. *The Competition for the Erection of the Nelson Monument Critically Examined*, London 1841. Goldicutt, it is true, refers to Roman coins rather than French prototypes for his designs, but this does not indicate an absence of French influence – merely an overriding respect for the Antique tradition. He mentions the partial adoption of his plan by Barry, thus suggesting an unfair procedure.

21. It is characteristic of the taste of the period that Canova's sculptures were reproduced with an English text and engraved by H. Moses in 1824.

22. cf. the present writer in *244*, op. cit., No. 5, p. 4 ff.

23. On Pugin, cf. M. Trappes-Lomax, *Pugin*, London 1932, and B. Ferrey, *Recollections of A. N. W. Pugin*, London 1861, Ph. Stanton, *Pugin*, London 1971.

24. cf. especially J. Martin, *Thames and Metropolis Improvement Plan*, London 1846, and *Plan of the London Connecting Railway*, London 1845. On Martin, cf. Th. Balston, *John Martin*, London 1934 and 1947, and *Projets* for a possible source of the artist's inspiration. J. Seznec, *John Martin en France*, London 1964.

25. No full monograph on Wyatville exists at the present time, but there is some scattered information, especially in connection with Benjamin Wyatt; the *Illustrations of Windsor Castle* edited by H. Ashton, London 1841, illustrates the architect's Gothic interests and gives some biographical data. cf. J. Britton, *Memoir of Sir Jeffrey Wyatville*, London 1834.

II

The Utopian Socialists

The term Utopian Socialists was coined by Karl Marx to denote a group of social thinkers whose attitude was unscientific and Utopian according to the dialectic method, because it based its hopes on the amelioration of the conditions of the working classes through individual benevolence and enterprise.[1] These thinkers belonged basically to the Age of Enlightenment, not only because they were born in the pre-Revolutionary period, but even more because they retained the optimistic belief in the efficacy of human choice and freedom of decision so characteristic of this age.

In Robert Owen's (1771–1858) plans for New Lanark, the development is primarily based on education; the 'Institution for the Formation of Character' opened on 1 January 1816 as a day-school for children and a night-school for adults, with special emphasis on music and dancing. Subsequently, he envisaged the building of villages of unity and co-operation, based on squares and subdivided into parallelograms, the line in the centre giving the site for the schools, the library, the lecture-room, the place of worship, the public kitchen and mess-rooms. Three of the sides were allotted to private apartments and the fourth to dormitories. Slight variations in planning existed, especially over the numbers of inhabitants, between the 'Report to the Committee of the Association for the Relief of the manufacturing and labouring poor' presented to the House of Commons in 1817 – showing villages intended for a population of 500 to 1,500, averaging about 1,000, and including a detailed view of the proposed layout – and the 'Report to the County of Lanark', submitted on 1 May 1820, which envisaged 300 to 2,000 people; the optimum numbers remained for Owen 800 to 1,200. Central heating of the type used in the Derby Infirmary was to be provided. The plans have in common: residence near the place of employment; communal living for the older children; and private lodging rooms for families of up to two children under three years of age. The basis of life was to be agricultural, but manufacture was to be added, in spite or because of Owen's own industrial experience, and so subsidiary buildings were to be found on the outskirts. Optimism and persuasion, to help the whole population of all classes to find happiness, was what Owen believed in.[2]

His desire for social betterment had been foreshadowed in

Original part of the New Lanark Mills.
(By courtesy of the British Nylon Spinners
Ltd., Pontypool)

John Bellers' *Proposals for Raising a College of Industry*, published
in 1696 and republished by Owen himself, whilst the taste for
architectural regularity in rural surroundings had been introduced to England with Gandy's circular satellite villages. It is
interesting to recall here that Owen was personally acquainted
with Jeremy Bentham and his preoccupations with the
'Panopticon'. Bentham was one of the partners in the New
Lanark enterprise: 'his only successful pecuniary speculation',
according to Dr Bowring. This may partly explain the Renaissance influence on Owen's designs, since Jeremy Bentham was
indebted to the Mannerist planners (as suggested above). A
link thus appears between formal reminiscences of the past
and a new humanitarian outlook coupled with an interest
in practical applications, an attitude which, in the case of
Bentham, is often – if rather one-sidedly – regarded as 'utilitarian'.

Whilst Bentham favoured the circle, Owen based his designs
on the square; the layout for his villages is similar to Ledoux's

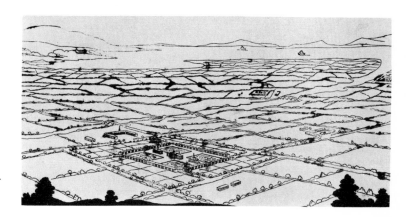

Owen, 'A View and Plan of the Agricultural and Manufacturing Villages of *Unity* and *Mutual Co-operation*'.

first plan for Chaux, not necessarily because of a direct derivation, but due to the prototypes employed.

F.-C.-M. Fourier (1772–1837) was concerned with harmony between the well-understood interests of the wealthy and the poor, based on the principles of association.[3] Whilst Owen believed in a paternalistic communism, Fourier sought community of consumption and production, but eschewed equality. The '*phalanstère*', the centre of the Fourier community, was to be a large building of three wings, open on one side, and enclosing an open space. The elevation of the phalanstery, with its emphasis on colonnades allowing for covered access to all parts of the building, presupposed Perrault's façade of the Louvre, the arcades of the Place de la Concorde and of the 18th-century part of the Palais Royal. The '*séristères*' were to contain the large halls necessitated by the '*séries passionnées*', the groups of members with diverging but complementary interests and emotions, and form part of the phalansteries.

It is worth noting that the three-sided 'court' was already

Fourier, Phalanstery; from *L'Avenir*.

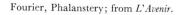

used by Owen for subsidiary buildings in his plan of 1817, but Fourier seems to have been unaware of this fact, or at any rate refused to acknowledge it, since he deprecated what he regarded as the Owenite square, known to him from the *Co-operative Magazine* of January 1826, where an indifferently drawn frontispiece shows the lay-out of New Harmony. Fourier published the plan for the *phalanstère* for the first time in *Le Nouveau Monde* in 1829, where numerous possible modifications in size and population are discussed, especially with reference to the recruitment of children, which he regarded as the third sex.

The plans of both thinkers have in common the accent on communal living, with women doing work outside the family circle and taking part in public life.[4] The basic contrast between the paternalistic, puritan attitude of Owen and the individualism and licence of Fourier overrides the similarities. For Fourier, the ideal city was to appear quite literally on this earth. The visionary element is particularized by a concern with economics, with optimum size and with the needs and numbers of the population. Fourier's *phalanstère* is designed for about 1,600–1,800 inhabitants of all ages, 1,620 being the theoretically correct figure; it is a sort of gigantic hotel, built in a shape reminiscent of the palace of Versailles. These structures were to be multiplied and improved over the years, and a number were to be built in the vicinity of each other. Fourier was aware of the activating influence of architecture on human occupations and relations and demanded variety and easy accessibility. His *séries passionnées* were divided into sub-sections, such as children, paupers, the middle class, the rich, and elected experts. Members' accommodation and shares differed in quality, and there was variety of occupation, too. The communities were to be based on horticulture and agriculture, reinforced by manufacture, although the scheme is rather vague with regard to the latter.

In England the ideal of the village community remained powerful. It was the pattern for William Thompson's co-operative agricultural settlements on Owenite lines. These were meant 'to obviate the enormous evils inseparable from the dense population of large towns', as expressed by Thompson in the *Co-operative Magazine* of July 1826.[5]

What was the English contribution to the theory of town-planning in the early 19th century? Robert Owen had already foreseen the breakdown of the cottage system, and wished to replace it with his villages of co-operation. But it is in Sidney Smirke that we find the first full acknowledgement of urban needs for all classes of inhabitant. He was intent on assisting the town dweller in his daily life and, according to the *Report from the Poor Law Commissioners to the House of Lords* of 1842 (Sessional

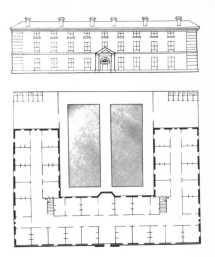

Plan for a Public Lodging House, after Sidney Smirke.

Papers), he was aware of the impracticability of finding sufficient land for the traditional cottages. Furthermore, he saw that what would now be called flats had an important positive contribution to make; 'buildings, placed under some public control, might be erected for the joint occupation of many families or individuals, and so arranged that each tenant might feel that he had the exclusive enjoyment of a home in the room or rooms which he occupied, and yet might partake, in common with his neighbours, of many important comforts and advantages now utterly unknown to him'. Thus Smirke also strove to preserve individualism, but within the community.

Report, Vol. XXVI, p. 272 ff.

On the other hand, J. C. Loudon's approach, as demonstrated in the same *Report*, was based on the traditional English cottage. He desired that the conditions laid down should be interpreted in a humane manner; in his own words, 'on the supposition that the intended builder of the cottage is actuated more by feelings of human sympathy than by a desire to make money'. These two examples should suffice to illustrate the spirit mainly animating the *Report*. The attitude taken in it was that improvement of the physical environment could be expected to elevate the mind.

Report, Vol. XXVI, p. 396 ff.

It may at first seem surprising that the Poor Law *Report* of 1842 gave scope to ideal plans, but closer consideration reveals that the social impulse which led to its preparation by Edwin Chadwick outgrew its immediate purpose, and, with the co-operation of architects, town-planning on a wider scale was envisaged. Characteristically, the impetus came from social thinkers rather than architects, who, when left to themselves, frequently studied the adaptations of historical styles and concentrated on single isolated buildings and their functional expression in past forms.

Owen's influence appears clearly in James Silk Buckingham's (1786–1855) ideas on co-operation and association. But he shows his independence in his book *National Evils and Practical Remedies*, published in London in 1849. The layout of the model town of Victoria, named after the Queen, is not for an 'Owenite village of co-operation', but represents an urban concept intended for 10,000 inhabitants. Victoria, to be built in the open country, was to be composed of numerous buildings, larger in the centre and gradually becoming smaller towards the outskirts, arranged in parallel rows on a quadrangular plan. The inhabitants were to lead a virtuous life and practise temperance. They were to be shareholders, and men, women and children were to shoulder work according to their strength and abilities.

J. S. Buckingham, Plan for the Model Town of Victoria.

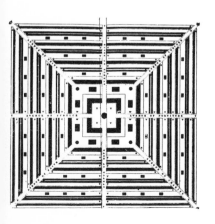

Buckingham's plan shows traces of his extensive travels, which included Italy and France as well as Eastern countries. The innermost square of Victoria is devoted to public build-

J. S. Buckingham, View of the Model Town of Victoria set in a landscape. [See p. 147.]

ings; the four outer rows of houses are graded to serve people of various incomes and vocations, the poorest classes to occupy the perimeter, since for them easy access to the open country appears particularly desirable. Buckingham's singularly ingenious device of adding covered galleries to the dwellings in order to allow social contacts in all weather, is indebted to Fourier's *phalanstère* and perhaps even more to the spacious bazaars of the Orient. The method of construction of these galleries was to be technically advanced, with iron supports and glass roofs foreshadowing the Crystal Palace.[6] Further modern features consisted of refectories for optional use, free medical attention and education, measures for smoke abatement, and the location of large factories outside the city to provide work for the unemployed.

A more rural ideal, based on the contribution of the workers, animated Robert Pemberton in his plans for a Happy Colony, which was to be in New Zealand, where land could be cheaply purchased. Here the foundations of 10 districts, each of 20,000 acres, could be easily laid. The circular plan was based on Chaux, on a misunderstanding of the perspective view in Ledoux's work suggesting a circle, when in fact the design is oval. Pemberton admired radial shapes, because 'all the grand forms in nature are round' and because they allowed free circulation. A miniature farm surrounded by four colleges was to be situated at the centre. In the inner ring terrestrial and celestial maps were to be laid out, and statues illustrating history erected in the groves.

The Colony was to be based on common ownership and the dignity of voluntary labour. Too much specialization and division of work was to be avoided, and thus the millennium would be quite literally reached. The first settlement was to be named 'Queen Victoria Town' because, like Buckingham, Pemberton was a loyal subject.[7]

The subsidiary buildings are allocated to radial routes, and open up the countryside in a manner reminiscent of Owen's villages. It is thus a true synthesis of the French and English traditions. This is corroborated by the text of the book, since the educational scheme, especially where it concerns children, is based on Owen, whilst the emphasis on the 'divine harmony of the passions' reflects Fourier's ideas.

Pemberton's plans are not only of historical significance, but remain of some topical interest even at the present time, since they seem to have influenced and form a link with the radial plan of Ebenezer Howard's Garden City.

The English ideal, as already suggested, remained the village: Blake's 'dark Satanic Mills' and William Morris's 'News from Nowhere', first published in the Journal of the Socialist League, *The Commonwealth*, in 1890, shared one basic attitude: distrust of the city. In Morris's opinion, London had

Centre of a Model Town, after Pemberton's plans for a Happy Colony.

ceased to exist as a large unit. 'We turned away from the river
at once, and were soon in the main road that runs through
Hammersmith. But I should have had no guess as to where I
was, if I had not started from the waterside; for King Street
was gone, and the highway ran through wide sunny meadows
and garden-like tillage.' Westminster Abbey and the Houses of
Parliament still stand and are preserved out of antiquarian
interest, but there is a 'splendid' market in Hammersmith, in a
building which embraced 'the best qualities of the Gothic of
Northern Europe with those of the Saracenic and Byzantine,
though there was no copying of any one of these styles'. Here
the eclectic style and the Romantic ideal of village life, grafted
on to a Socialist outlook, form an unexpected and highly individual synthesis, but they offer no solution to the problems
of the contemporary town-planner.[8]

In the last years of the 19th century and the early decades of
the 20th, a significant change can be observed, not so much in
the attitude of the planners, but in those writers who deal with
Utopias. Previously the typical Utopia was positive and to a
large extent a town-planner's vision; now, as seen clearly in
H. G. Wells's *When the Sleeper Wakes*, published in 1899, the
giant city becomes enlarged, like a 'mechanized beehive'. The
architecture is overwhelming, suspension bridges are flung over
chasms, whilst many activities are carried on underground.
Furthermore, the roofing of the town is continuous, and the
latter is enclosed by huge walls. These characteristics are
regarded by Wells as negative, since he still subconsciously
accepted the rural ideal.[9]

A similar attitude underlies the work of Patrick Geddes
(1854–1932) and Frank Lloyd Wright (1869–1959). Both
showed a marked individualism, linked with a belief in the per-
fectibility of man, even if their achievement was not strictly in
the physical planning of towns. For Geddes the chief concern
was with his immediate, although changing, environment; the
hic et nunc of his detailed preoccupations singles him out as a
realist. Lewis Mumford, who has added the term 'cotechnic' to
Geddes's 'paleotechnic' and 'neotechnic', perhaps gives a
clearer assessment of the Geddesian vision than the authentic,
scattered writings. To quote Mumford: 'Geddes was a teacher,
and like all great teachers, from Socrates onward, he relied
upon direct intercourse rather than the printed word.' In this
trait, Geddes reminds one of Boullée, who, like him, was a
thinker and designer rather than an architectural planner. The
form of the image eems to have eluded Geddes, however; his
approach was rational rather than visual, and as a result the
buildings erected under his influence, though functional, are
architecturally undistinguished.[10]

By contrast, Mumford's approach is based on an ideal of

garden cities which influences his choice of examples and his historical approach. He idealizes or criticizes the past by referring to the demands he makes for the present and the future.

Frank Lloyd Wright was primarily concerned with the relationship between landscape or region and an individually sited architecture.[11] He had a deep dislike and distrust of existing cities with their unwieldy proportions, and his architectural sensitivity shrank from indifferent and ugly buildings. His ideal was the negation of the city, as the name 'Broad Acre' implies; he was a believer in the isolated life of the individual amidst nature, a concept which, to our mind, is inapplicable to small countries and overlooks the gregariousness of human beings who, from choice or necessity, choose to live in communities. For example, the function of the village well, apparent to Geddes, was ignored by Wright. He represents a contradiction, in that he can be regarded as an anarchist planner; it is this inherent contradiction that gives a special flavour to works which, designed for the few and wealthy, are meant to contribute to the solution of the problems of large conurbations and capital cities.

Ebenezer Howard (1850–1928) struggled in isolation for a solution to pressing town-planning problems. He coined the term 'Garden City', first found in his programmatic book, *Tomorrow: A Peaceful Path to Social Reform*, published in 1898; here an ideal of low density park and garden development and small townships was formulated, possibly influenced by

Ebenezer Howard, Diagram of a Garden City. From *Garden Cities of Tomorrow*, London 1902.

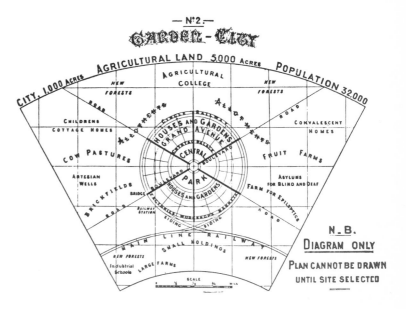

Pemberton's 'Happy Colony'. This was a creative reaction
against the squalor engendered by the Industrial Revolution.
How far these conceptions are equally applicable to present-day
needs is a different problem, aggravated by the fact that
Howard has been frequently misunderstood by his own followers, who overlooked the basic regularity of his diagrams, his
emphasis on agriculture, on the proximity of places of work to
residential quarters, and on the interpenetration of rural and
urban life. His claim to originality among planners rests on the
singular emphasis on liberty found in his work – a liberty which
he believed was preferable to equality. His diagram of the
Garden City is based on concentric circles and is to be used as a
universal rather than a particular model, since the 'plan cannot
be drawn until site selected'. The social principle to be applied
was to rule out private gain: all ground rents were to be paid to
Trustees for a Central Council.[12]

Octavia Hill (1838–1912), the only woman to have emerged
so far from a survey of thinkers on town-planning, was pre-
eminently of her time, the Victorian era. It is interesting how,
in her circumscribed world, she seems to have had no knowledge of either Engels' writings on *The Condition of the Working
Class in England in 1844*, or Ebenezer Howard's ideas expressed
in his book *To-Morrow*, which appeared in 1898.[13] What is
striking is her real interest in the poor, her self-assured conviction that she had a duty to 'rule her tenants', and her
preference for cottages rather than 'courts', the term then
applied to multi-storeyed housing. She was thus less open-
minded than Sidney Smirke, for example.

Contemporary Tendencies

Tony Garnier's design for an Industrial City, planned in
1901, now justly famous, is distinguished not so much in its
detail but in the emphasis on the factory and the frank acknowledgement of the industrial scene.[14] The medieval linear village
is a possible prototype, although no conscious derivation is
apparent; neither is a relationship to be seen with the linear
new town, as designed in the second half of the 18th century by
James Craig for Edinburgh, for example.[15] The extension of
the principle to the whole town and the industrial emphasis
on zoning are Garnier's own, and the '*Ville Radieuse*' of Le
Corbusier (1887–1965) is derived from here. Garnier's emphasis on zoning has had a strong and perhaps dangerous
influence; it is based on a view which divides life in general, and
human activities in particular, into separate compartments,
understandably so when the 'dark Satanic Mills' were
threatening, but out of date in a period in which schools and
well-built factories have much in common. However, the
concept of the linear town may well be adaptable to future

planning in large and sparsely populated regions, since it opens up the countryside and provides easy communication.

It might seem an over-simplification to concentrate on Sant'Elia, the Italian protagonist of Futurism, as the sole or chief exponent of the reaction against the village ideal and the emphasis on technology. But certain tendencies are crystallized and clarified in his work which, although not unique, are formulated and emphasized in a particularly forceful and telling manner.[16] Also, the fact that futurism developed in Italy was no matter of chance: in a progressive country possessing a rich historical heritage, a conscious reaction against historicism took place, the affirmation of novel, formal and technical tendencies. The open acknowledgement that form had to follow material function was a positive factor in overcoming the limitations of this historicism, since, on the basis of simplicity, a new, contemporary and powerful idiom could be created. This counter-movement can be most clearly seen in Italy, but it has parallels in the leading architectural centres of Europe.

The Russian Constructivists must be remembered for combining in their work a commitment to social values, with new structural ideas. Their planning can be regarded as dialectic, for they not only set out to improve the lot of the urban worker, but at the same time eschewed the overgrown city. Here ideal planning was an effective force, which ended abruptly for political reasons.[17]

The situation in Russia was not unlike conditions in Germany after defeat in World War I, when the activities of the Bauhaus group, concerned with the total environment, were related to those of the Constructivists. Hannes Meyer, in charge of architecture at the Bauhaus from 1929 to 1930, actually left Germany to work in Russia, where he stayed until 1936.[18]

Returning to Italy, Sant'Elia presents in his designs and writings the triumph of bare mechanization over natural function: the large city; he advocates the 'Megalopolis', which Lewis Mumford found so repugnant, as the operating principle. He extols a town for robots who want to move, although no aim for this movement is apparent. The stress laid on the transient and the dynamism of architectural form, gives the impression almost of secularized Gothic; this is detached from human need for shelter, affection and survival. Sant'Elia only caters for man as a one-sided being. 'We must invent and remake the Futurist city like an immense assembly yard, dynamic in every part . . . we must abolish decoration.'

Sant'Elia's personal poignancy and vehemence may be partially explained as an individual reaction against the overwhelming past of his native Italy, a past which by its very quality proved stifling for a dissatisfied generation in revolt. He

R. Banham in the *Architectural Review*, May 1955, p. 297.

designed a skyscraper with airports, underground dwellings and
pathways, in which the desire for seclusion and the need for
privacy had been ignored or superseded. The *Unité d'Habitation*,
as envisaged by Le Corbusier, is unthinkable without this
precedent.[19]

The greatness of Le Corbusier's conception of a '*ville
contemporaine*', an up-to-date town for three million inhabitants,
still reflects the Classical tradition. The plan was exhibited in
the Salon d'Automne of 1922 in Paris, and shows a square
inscribed in a rectangle. It includes three triumphal arches for
the main approaches and provides for expansion by including a
landscaped garden, a *jardin anglais*, which could be replaced at
a later date. The most static element is perhaps the rigid zoning
envisaged in the four parts: a centre, urban housing, a development area and garden cities. The civic buildings with their
cupolas are reminiscent of the tradition most clearly epitomized
by Boullée's architecture, and form a significant contrast to
the high skyscrapers.

The model of the *Ville Radieuse* of 1935 comes more to terms
with reality, and forms the basis of numerous similar designs for
individual cities, and for the re-planning of Paris. Here the
emphasis is on the skyscraper in a park setting, and stress is
laid on the use of glass and simplicity of form. The corridor
street has disappeared completely, and vertical garden cities –
as Le Corbusier called them – save space and allow for free
circulation. The development in height is indebted to Sant'Elia,
whilst the underlying symmetry is characteristic of the French
architectural tradition. To these formal considerations is also
added interest of a social nature, centred on the individual
dwelling in the English manner with an awareness of the varying
needs of all classes of society, at least in theory if not so much in
practice.

The adaptability of Le Corbusier's designs to new purposes,
and their utilitarian value, has been questioned. This criticism
cannot, however, be sustained, since a great architect producing
original solutions can hardly be expected to foresee all future
contingencies.[20] Indeed, as a rule the history of art is as much
one of patrons as of artists. The planner of ideal cities occupies
a rather singular position in that he can dispense with this
factor. He is allowed freedom of vision, but at the same time
the lack of realization limits his contribution. His plans act as
regulative models, rather than architectural contributions.

During recent years the stature of Le Corbusier has continued to grow, especially when seen in an historical perspective. His two outstanding articles, '*Urbanisme*' of 1923 and
'*Vers une architecture nouvelle*' of 1925, already expressed the credo
of functionalism in its most succinct form, with the house a
'*machine à habiter*' and the definition of the tool as a vital

element in planning: *L'outillage, ce qui sert*. In spite of this, the use of the tool and the machine is embodied in a wide vision for Le Corbusier, and his standards are perfectionist in terms of form as well as of content. His abortive designs for an international centre, the 'Mundaneum' in Geneva, and the project for a World City, *La cité mondiale* outside that city, both of 1929, illustrate his concern with the ideal rather than the day-to-day aims of architecture. They are characteristic of his creative spirit, the spirit of a man who, in spite of international recognition and imitation, was frustrated in his aspirations towards multi-national and classless communities.

When comparing Garnier's *Cité Industrielle*, Sant'Elia's Futurist Town, and Le Corbusier's *Ville Radieuse*, their similarities are more apparent than their differences. They dispense clearly with the enclosures and minimize the outstanding civic buildings in the centre, thus breaking new ground. At the same time they lose the cohesion and simplicity of the urban pattern. It is interesting that the Garden City of Ebenezer Howard is more traditional in this sense, and continues, at any rate in diagrammatic form, the emphasis on the city core and its circular boundaries. The stress laid on the common use and possession of land also links this concept with those of the Utopian Socialists. That the garden suburb sprang from the Garden City is one of the ironies of architectural history.

When Indra's daughter in Strindberg's *Dream Play* came down to earth bringing her gifts, she found that the recipients were disillusioned by them; the green rod was not of the right green. In other words, a desired objective may prove disappointing, if received at the wrong moment, under altered circumstances, or when taste has changed. Today town-planning provokes this kind of reaction. The inhabitants of new towns discover their shortcomings; the suburbs are regarded as dormitories; city centres become denuded; and the sprawl over the open countryside continues. Planners who believe in the city as a focus of social life are still only partly effective; but their impact is growing and makes itself felt on the most hardened adherents of low density building, and garden suburbs. [21.]

This study is an historical one; it is concerned neither with prophecy nor propaganda, but with the living past and with the influence of ideal images on architectural achievement. Correctly understood, ideal planning cannot disappoint, simply because it represents ideals rather than blue-prints for action. Indeed, when executed, ideal plans become trivialized and coarsened. In Marxian terms, qualitative change is quantified, as opposed to quantity turning into quality.[22.] If, however, ideal plans are taken as regulative models, they represent the prevalent aspirations of their age. A clear realization of the functions of the city, and an expression of these aims in a manner which acknowledges the necessity of absolute standards are important, even if the attainment of them is permanently out of reach. In this context, the ideal plan functions as a corrective as well as a challenge. However, one should not forget that what are regarded as principles of town-planning in an absolute sense are frequently only principles of contemporary planning. [23.]

Nevertheless, so much is certain: town-planning expresses the social background and the attitudes or evaluations of the dominant sectors of society. This was demonstrated by the views of Hitler and his architects who encouraged a de-humanizing and massive architecture, stressing axial symmetry in a void. The projected elevations are top-heavy, so that the spectator is oppressed by their looming weight, as well as lost in the vast spaces.[25] Another point to remember is that in a hierarchical society the basis of patronage is narrowed, whilst in an egalitarian society it is widened.

The utilitarian attitude usually presented by the middle classes forms a contrast to the spirit of the various dedicated settlements, especially in the United States, where the reconciliation of the communal spirit with the exigencies of everyday life was attempted. [24.]

Ideal planning differs from town-planning because it can largely dispense with the influence of the patron. This is both its strength and its weakness. In the past it has been mostly static, but the ideal plan of the future will have to be dynamic and allow for change.

Is there a difference between an Ideal City and a Utopia? These terms, when loosely used, are interchangeable; but, defined more closely, the Utopia as interpreted by Karl Mannheim[26] presupposes violent change, whilst the planner of ideal cities is a reformer within his given society and locality. For this reason Boullée and Ledoux had no wish to follow the political revolutionary trends, and the latter went to prison rather than conform. In the political sphere the same facts appear: the Communist states are by no means the most progressive in town-planning, whilst Holland, Sweden and Finland are in the vanguard of contemporary developments.

In the future, emphasis will inevitably be laid on redeeming the city centres, and on re-housing in areas within easy reach of these. By such means, cultural life, which is now so seriously handicapped by long journeys to and from work, may again be stimulated, and the vast conurbations should develop a new creative impetus as far as the theatre, cultural meetings and social gatherings are concerned.

Perhaps the most doubtful feature of contemporary planning is over-rigid zoning, which in effect separates the place of work from housing and so breaks up the continuity of life. Furthermore, it should not be overlooked that any planning which segregates the poorer from the richer strata of the population diminishes social integration, and therefore constitutes an aggravating rather than a positive factor, however important it may be as a short-term policy to relieve those most in need.

Over-emphasis on zoning and the problems of over-crowding aggravate chaotic and unsatisfactory conditions within many of the older cities, but this presupposes in effect small and manageable units, such as characterized the medieval towns. Indeed, it is startling to see how, from the Middle Ages onwards, after a short interlude during the periods of the Baroque and the Enlightenment, it was the provincial township or village which remained the ideal, especially in England. By contrast, the city in glass and concrete was developed with formal and technical problems in mind, but it neglected the human element, the inhabitant. Even in the work of Le Corbusier, and this in spite of the lavish provision of amenities in blocks of flats, there is frequently no definition of the city's core, which can be continuously expanded by additional buildings.

A contemporary answer to traffic problems is found in the plan of Brasilia, the new capital of Brazil, by Lucio Costa. The

Caricature by Paul Strøyer, showing a children's playground surrounded by traffic. (*R.I.B.A. Journal*, September 1961)

layout is based on a cross, allowing for up-to-date traffic
fly-overs. A slight inclination of the ground is the basis of an
extended crescent, articulated by squares forming one of the
axes, while the other artery terminates in an equilateral triangle
housing the government offices.[27] It is perhaps characteristic
that a new solution should be found in a vast and young country
rather than in Europe, where the old capitals have grown over
the centuries. The plan is the outcome of a national competition
with an international jury, showing how successful such a
venture can be in fostering talent and imaginative designs.

During recent years Sweden has been in the forefront of
urban development. There the current appeal is less to idealism
than to an intelligent appraisal of contemporary social needs.
The cost of building new railway lines, roads, parking places
and sewers is regarded as a basic factor in the concentration of
fairly autonomous satellite towns of the Vällingby and Farsta
type, but these material considerations lead to compact and
mixed developments, in which the university professor – at
least in theory – can live in the same block as the postman.
Even if the parents do not as yet mix, the majority of children
attend the same schools, and so social integration is hoped for
in the future.

The playgrounds with their 'play' sculpture and youth
centres form part of the integral planning. The quality of
individual buildings is not always outstanding – less so than in
Denmark, for instance – but architectural problems are solved
in a manner both monumental and functional. Indeed, until
recently, anyone interested in a mixed economy could do no
better than become acquainted with Sweden, where 'planning
for freedom', in the words of the late Professor K. Mannheim,
is attempted. A combination of civic enterprise and private
practice ensures flexibility and individual variations.[28]

The landscape background and the rigours of the winter in
Sweden may go far to explain the prevalent feeling for simple
shapes and precise volume. It is significant in this context that
the models which were preferred in architectural schools and
town planners' offices are in white to clarify the forms, thus
evoking a winter landscape.

Whether the towns and cities of the future will again be
clearly defined by borders such as green belts – not necessarily
walls – is at present impossible to decide, but some of Alvar
Aalto's buildings for the Civic Centre in Säynätsalo show
an appreciation of the long tradition of enclosure with their
changing levels and circumscribed spaces.[29]

The ancient function of physical protection always had its
spiritual counterpart, as shown by the crown of walls of the
goddess Tyche. But the psychological effect of enclosure gains
in importance at the present time, because there are no walls

'Play' sculpture in the Humlegården, Stockholm.

against modern weapons. By a reverse process, they protect the country from the encroachment of the town. It seems unnecessary to look to infantile reminiscences for the explanation of this longing for enclosure. A town is not an overgrown womb. The search for security and stability expressed by the enclosed town is an adult response. The 'over-extension' of living space, still so popular today, may therefore be a retrograde rather than an advanced phase of evolution. Adaptability should not be confused with formlessness. The sprawling city with its extended communications makes social and family contact casual and intermittent; the generations are separated by a gulf not only of experience and time, but also of space, and this is a barrier to social integration.[30] For this reason, the large and compact city may well be the future ideal form in Europe. This applies equally to Great Britain but not necessarily to large and rapidly developing countries, such as Australia or the Soviet Union, where the linear city, as designed by Garnier, may still have much to commend it.

A similar principle is seen in the interior and exterior of buildings. The 18th-century *enfilade* of rooms is replaced by the open plan, whilst the processional way is abandoned for

the unexpected and for irregular spaces. But the aesthetic
advantages of symmetry are being rediscovered. Certainly,
well-balanced – though asymmetrical – buildings can appear
satisfying, but a basic human urge is reflected in a desire for
symmetry, which is based on the human form. The larger the
scale the more pronounced is this necessity.

Together with the wish for symmetry may go a renewed
desire for painting and sculpture. At the present time, factories
often look like schools, and schools almost like factories. That is
satisfactory to a point, and illustrates that the fetish made of
zoning is no longer necessary. Since modern factories can be
beautiful as well as hygienic, there is no reason why people
should live away from them. Similarly, flats can be provided
as part of office blocks, a new type of city planning now
encouraged by some local authorities within the Greater
London Conurbation.

A sympathetic insight into the progress of planning may
not only affect those immediately concerned; the ramifications
lead further. Planning may help to break the isolation of the
contemporary artist and give him a renewed interest in the
social purpose which is contained in, or expressed by, the plan.
Thus a link between the artist and his public may be re-
established, a link which gave support to creative activity in the
past, and may again in the future lead to inspiration. The sole
criterion of individual originality as a yardstick of appreciation
can now be replaced by an understanding of the purpose expressed: in other words, by a sense of social value.

Kadleigh, Project for High Paddington.

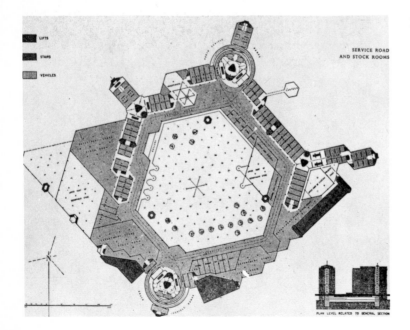

It would be futile to compare developments in the theory of architecture with the concepts characteristic of nuclear physics and the expanding horizons of astronomy; however, the location of large structures underground combined with lofty 'high rise' blocks of imposing scale, based on elaborate calculations, shows an affinity with the dynamism of scientific theory. Sergei Kadleigh's 'town for 8,000 people', a project for High Paddington, as well as his Barbican scheme, cogently express the inter-related and interdependent levels of a comprehensive vision which may well be regarded as a contemporary image of an ancient ideal of the city – that of integrating housing with industry and trade.[31]

Once tall blocks become typical rather than exceptional, an emphasis on lower buildings gains in importance as an aesthetic contrast, as seen in an outstanding historical example in Greenwich, where the small-scale Queen's House is emphasized by the framing towers of the Royal Naval Hospital. An adaptation of this principle seems applicable to some of the blighted European towns, where high blocks on the outskirts might provide a wall-like enclosure, whilst the centre could consist of lower civic buildings, a reversal of the usual present-day practice. The open spaces thus secured would allow not only for park development, but also for individual gardens and even allotments, if they were desired.

As the late Karl Mannheim suggested in his *Diagnosis of Our Time*,[32] European civilization is confronted with a choice and, unless this is widely and unambiguously made, the town-planner will have no public backing and will therefore be forced to work in a vacuum. Obviously the same solutions are not applicable to all circumstances; Holland provides examples for England which deserve careful study. Not only are a similarity of climate and the constant challenge of the sea found there, but in many ways the way of life conforms to kindred values. Furthermore, the destruction of Rotterdam has afforded a great opportunity for redeeming the centre of an obsolescent city. It has to be borne in mind, however, that the Dutch have a greater sense of equality, whilst paradoxically the existing differences of class and caste are more pronounced than in England. To give a concrete example: the communal enclosed squares of contemporary housing in Holland might well incorporate suggestions for English planning, especially since the square is a traditional element of the urban scene in England.

Generally speaking, the communal facilities of clubs, community centres, housing estates and flats, have as yet not been fully explored, or if so explored, not put into practice. Surely they afford possibilities to reconcile the needs of individual privacy with the claims of a shared and integrated life.

Model for the re-planning of the Cool-
singel, Rotterdam. (Photograph: Openbare Werken, Rotterdam)

It is a common experience that in order to reach the possible
the impossible has to be attempted, or, to put it another way, a
society and its members largely live on hope. Because of this,
European society has not only been maintained, but has expanded. In spite of drastic social change, total disruption has
been avoided.

The situation today represents a particular challenge. Many
people have lost hope. In *The Costs of Economic Growth*, E. J.
Mishan cogently expresses a keen sense of disillusion with the
urban environment, more and more threatened by the private
motor-car: 'Men have become the victims of their faith in
progress.' Mishan questions the benefits of industrial expansion
and improvements in trade. The superficial optimism of the
planner is replaced by a sense of doom, widespread because at
present difficulties accumulate and no ready solutions are in
sight.[33] He warns against isolating the old from the young, and
by implication opposes zoning as a fetish. However, zoning has
recently been superseded as a focus of attention by problems of
transportation: movement and speed take the place of concentration and repose, thus negating the civic function of the
city. In these circumstances, the concept of the ideal city
becomes rather more than less of a challenge, as the ideal plan
can retain its value even if its adaptation disappoints.

To fill the ensuing void appeals are made to snobbery, and a
formalistic acceptance of current values may replace conviction.
If these attitudes should influence town-planners, the prospects
for the future seem depressing indeed. But historical processes
can go into reverse: powers of renewal fostered by changing
political, economic and individual circumstances may emerge,

interpreted by a 'freed' personal will, freed that is from solely selfish and short-sighted considerations.

The current task is to combine in a true synthesis a sense of communion and social responsibility with respect for privacy and individuality. The feeling of solitude, frequently found when family relationships' have broken up for internal or external reasons, has to be dispelled by finding contacts for isolated people. Plans have to be varied, dynamic and flexible, allowing for future changes and personal adaptations.

In surveying retrospectively the evolution of European town-planning, one is struck by its variety and dynamism, factors which tend towards social integration and welfare. These characteristics shaped the forms employed and determined their development. They also served to give unity and cohesion to complex and seemingly contradictory developments, which have led from a desire for perfection in the past to a new emphasis on experiment and technical achievement.

As far as the intent of city-planning is universal, it is based on the simplest geometric forms, but variations issue logically from changing social requirements. As a rule, the city possesses a central core which includes the main piazza; the boundary is emphasized by a border, either of walls or of avenues, or a green belt, as a means of demarcation. The exceptions are so few – among them plans by Garnier and early Le Corbusier – that although they are of great sociological and aesthetic significance, they have so far not altered the main trends of development. Indeed, Le Corbusier's master-plan for Chandigarh, or Costa's Brasilia, return to a more Classical tradition.

While the Classical tradition in architecture and planning is still alive in southern Europe, northern Europe favours the grown or organic city, a challenge to the regular plan. However, simple and symmetrical lay-outs are still regarded as the norm against which the picturesque elements are set.

Ideal cities are distinguished by regular geometric patterns, especially the circle and the square, both of which form the basis for an intelligent appreciation. The Indian *mandala* symbol combines paradoxically the infinite flow of the circular outline with the finite regularity of enclosed space, a design which engenders a feeling of harmony. In contrast, the polygon appears less perfect because of its angularity. The square, also a regular finite form, signifies repose, whereas the globe represents movement. The Monument in Goethe's garden in Weimar, which consists of a sphere erected upon a cube, is a telling example of this.[34]

It is impossible to predict how far the more flexible plans of the future will allow for expansion without the blurring of the city outline. It seems to emerge from the present study, however,

Above
Soleri, 'Arcosanti' (section), showing Neo-Classical influence.
(By courtesy of the Editor, *Architectural Association Quarterly*)

Left
Soleri, City in the form of a Hexahedron. (By courtesy of the
Editor, *Architectural Association Quarterly*)

that multi-focal planning will still retain its basic traditional
characteristics, and therefore forms of the past may well act as
a stimulus for further developments.

Flexibility will have to be applied not only to elevations and
densities but also to problems of communication and traffic
congestion, problems which have attained an urgency at the
present totally absent in the past.[35] Indeed, if an over-rigid
fixed pattern is not imposed, the countryside may be enhanced
rather than defiled by building.

The dynamic conception of an expanding town, using the
simplest geometric forms, the circle and the square, is emphasized by Doxiadis,[36] whose ideal concept includes regional
planning for up to 90 million people, with a multiplicity of
focal points in an open-ended conurbation. By contrast,
Paolo Soleri particularly stresses 'miniaturization', a variety
of individually conceived, compact projects, some of considerable size. Equally, his ideas on interiorization rather
than expansion contribute to a concern for the preservation
of land, and an understanding of the contrast between nature
and the built environment. His work on *Arcology*,[37] a combination of the concepts of architecture and ecology, is, in
spite of innovations, still steeped in the Neo-Classical tradition.
Whether he develops his plans in height or depth, such as in
his 'Noahs' or 'Babels', they express a sense of regularity and

symmetry coupled with a concern for meticulous detail.

Nowadays, architects are consulted on an international scale. It is therefore unavoidable that, in spite of regional, social, religious and individual differences, a universal style is emerging. This is no novelty, since great architectural styles have transcended national and regional limitations in the past. The main difference now is that the means of communication have accelerated contacts, and the globe of the earth has become one. The plans should be flexible, however, allowing for changes in social structure and the use and development of land. No doubt women will play an ever-growing part in that evolution, and this on an international scale; by extending their perennial personal sphere, they will be enabled to make the world at large more fully their home.[38] Indeed, the possible significance of a different division of labour and its architectural implications are far-reaching, as can be seen, for example, in the Israeli communal settlements, or Kibbutzim.[39]

Now that international communications make a universal conception of the city almost inevitable, the emphasis on the uniqueness of siting and the importance of varying social backgrounds are being consciously emphasized. It was in the small and confined communities of the past that the town-planner conceived the notion of the ideal city; now it is the adaptation of the universal vision to the particular issue which is gaining significance. The benefits of satisfactory conditions of living escape statistics, whilst the harm done by slums is clearly apparent. Nevertheless, the powers of the positive aspects of environment are as important as the evil elements and, if the right questions are asked, lessons may be learned from history. The questions may be subjective, but not the answers, if facts are respected. 'What ought to surprise and gratify us is the extent to which the spirit of objectivity has won its triumphs.'[40]

We have reviewed the evolution of images of ideal cities in three phases: the religious, the geometrically formal and the social. From the evidence it would appear that the latter has not as yet been fully realized; thus interaction between the principles of town-planning and the demands of daily life should lead to novel solutions in the future.

Pride in progress has stimulated visions of the ideal city. At the same time a critical attitude has persisted, which is seen in Antiquity in connection with Babylon, the evil city, and is found in Cobbett's strictures on the 'great wen' of London; more recently, it has appeared in Spengler's and Mumford's criticism of 'Megalopolis', and a similar attitude is implied in Sir Herbert Read's positive evaluation of small cultural units.[41] However, in spite of this, cities are continuing to grow.

The planner now endeavours to overcome the pitfalls of

Zadkine, Statue symbolizing the Resurgence of Rotterdam (1951). (Photograph: Openbare Werken, Rotterdam) [See p. 166.]

mass concentration, and to find means of decentralization within the larger unit. A conscious emphasis on activities, community centres, libraries and places of entertainment is part of an evolution which, starting in the Renaissance, was stimulated and enriched by the Classical Reformers and is still in process at the present time.

The ideal image of the city was envisaged by the Greeks in the form of a woman in repose. In contrast, Ossip Zadkine's monumental statue of 1951, dedicated to the liberation of Rotterdam, appears dynamic. The figure was erected in the heart of the town, near the harbour and the shopping centre. Here the powers of destruction and their failure to overcome the resurgent hope of the unconquered city are expressed in an abstract style.

The two contrasting elements, the garden city and the mechanized town, constitute our contemporary heritage from which the town-planner has to choose, either by attempting a compromise, or by a selective application from these seemingly exclusive prototypes. At the present time, awareness of weaknesses in modern planning is increasing. How cities, if they survive, are to be built in the year 2000 is a topical problem.[42] The diagnosis of ills is easy; the cure difficult. But essentially a wish exists to maintain the city as a social centre to integrate neighbourhoods and preserve historical continuity.

'La ville est morte: vive la ville!' may well be a rallying cry for the future.

---

1. On the term Utopian Socialists, cf. M. Buber, *Paths in Utopia*, London 1949. The present writer is unable to follow the grouping of the material, whilst accepting the main conclusions. Also L. Mumford, *The Story of Utopias*, London 1923. Ch. Gide and Ch. Rist, *History of Economic Doctrines*, numerous translations and editions, 2nd ed. London 1961, p. 308.

2. R. Owen, *New View of Society*, London 1818. Also *Report to the County of Lanark*, Glasgow 1821, and many other writings. G. D. H. Cole, *Robert Owen*, London 1925, *passim*. M. Cole, *Robert Owen*, London 1953, *passim*.

3. F.-C.-M. Fourier, *Le Nouveau Monde*, Paris 1829, especially p. 146, for the plan. V. Considérant in *L'Avenir*, Bordeaux, n.d., but after the death of Fourier on 10 October 1837. This work may be connected with Considérant's *Considérations sociales sur l'architectonique*, Paris 1834, unfortunately not available for this study. For a cursory survey, cf. Lavedan III, p. 77 ff.

4. On the changing position of women, cf. H. Rosenau, *Woman in Art*, London 1944, and V. Klein, *The Feminine Character*, London 1946. Present trends of population in the less developed countries may well change with the emancipation of women, and lead to restriction in the size of families, so that town-planners will be able to concentrate on more stable figures, rather than rising ones. cf. also K. Millett, *Sexual Politics*, New York 1970.

5. cf. R. K. P. Pankhurst, *William Thompson*, London 1954, especially p. 133 f.

6. Buckingham's study is of particular significance because of its detailed emphasis on the most up-to-date building techniques of his time.

7. R. Pemberton, *The Happy Colony*, London 1854, p. 80. S. Lang, *Architectural*

Review, August 1952, op. cit. It is true that Ledoux had some influence on Pemberton, but it is much slighter than suggested by Dr Lang, since Chaux was projected as an oval, while the Happy Colony was designed on a circular lay-out.

8. cf. H. Jackson, *On Art and Socialism*, London 1947.

9. R. Gerber, *Utopian Fantasy*, London 1955, *passim*. I am indebted for this reference to Professor D. M. White. cf. also A. L. Morton, *The English Utopia*, London 1952, and Berneri, op. cit., *passim*. M. Holloway, *Heavens on Earth*, London 1951, contains a reproduction of the Owenite community by T. S. Whitwell. L. Mumford, *The Story of Utopias*, London 1923.

10. Ph. Boardman, *Patrick Geddes*, Introduction by Lewis Mumford, University of North Carolina Press 1944, p. viii. cf. also *Town Planning Review*, 1912, p. 176 ff. and 1913, p. 78 ff. L. Mumford, especially his pioneering work *The Culture of Cities*, London 1938. Also J. Gottmann, *Megalopolis*, New York 1961.

11. F. L. Wright, *The Future of Architecture*, London 1953.

12. How popular Howard's attitude still remains is well illustrated by L. B. Keeble in *Town and Country Planning*, June 1957, p. 241 ff. cf. C. B. Purdom, *The Building of Satellite Towns*, London 1949. A good and succinct survey of the problems involved is found in C. Stewart, *A Prospect of Cities*, London 1952, especially with regard to Saltaire and kindred developments. A warmly intelligent approach to the problem is shown in E. Denby, *Europe Re-housed*, London 1938, which still contains many topical facts. For a comprehensive survey, cf. L. B. Keeble, *Principles and Practice of Town and Country Planning*, London 1952.

13. It is regrettable that the biographies of Octavia Hill are undiluted hagiography; her personality deserves a fuller assessment. cf. C. E. Maurice, *Life of Octavia Hill*, London 1913, and E. H. C. M. Bell, *Octavia Hill*, London 1942. On Engels' views of housing in Britain, cf. the recent edition of W. O. Henderson and W. H. Chaloner, *The Condition of the Working Class in England in 1844*, Oxford 1958, and their criticism of the sources of this indictment. It should be noted that Engels offers no positive contribution to the re-planning of industrial cities.

14. T. Garnier, *Une Cité industrielle*, Paris 1918, but already projected in 1901. Also G. Vernesi, *T. Garnier*, Milan 1948, and Th. Sharp, *Town Planning*, revd. ed., 1945, p. 45. Also Lavedan III, *passim*. cf. also D. Wiebenson, *Tony Garnier: The Cité Industrielle*, New York 1969.

15. On the development of the Linear and Lineal City, cf. Th. Sharp, op. cit. The term Linear City was coined by the Spaniard Arturo Sorio y Mata in 1882. Tony Garnier's *Cité* still possessed a definite centre in spite of its linear outline. His interest in public and civic buildings is abundantly proved by his achievement at Lyons.

16. On Holland, cf. H. L. C. Jaffé, *De Stijl*, Amsterdam and London 1956; R. Banham on 'Sant'Elia' in *Architectural Review*, May 1955, p. 295 ff., and June 1956, p. 343 ff. F. L. Wright, *The Future of Architecture*, New York 1953 and London 1955. That Frank Lloyd Wright is not dealt with in this study is due not to lack of recognition of his greatness, but only to the fact that his work seems more concerned with the individual building than with the town as a whole, and this may well be characteristic of the present American way of life. cf. J. M. Fitch, *American Building*, London n.d. Among the almost forgotten pioneers, E. Hönig's designs of *c.* 1935 have to be mentioned, especially regarding buildings with sloping ramps and the elimination of staircases.

17. A. Kopp, *Ville et révolution*, Paris 1967. English translation London 1970, *Town and Revolution*, and also *Art in Revolution*, Arts Council Exhibition 1971.

18. W. M. Wingler, *Das Bauhaus*, Bramsche 1968. C. Naylor, *The Bauhaus*, London 1968.

19. On Le Corbusier and P. Jeanneret, cf. *Œuvre complète*, numerous editions. Also M. Gautier, *Le Corbusier*, Paris 1944.

20. On Le Corbusier, cf. also S. Papadaki, *Le Corbusier*, New York 1948. On the classical tradition, E. Kaufmann, *Von Ledoux bis Le Corbusier*, Vienna 1933, and J. Gantner, *Revision der Kunstgeschichte. Prolegomena zu einer Kunstgeschichte*, with an Appendix on Semper and Le Corbusier, Vienna 1932.

21. S. Florence in *The Metropolis in Modern Life*, New York 1955, Columbia University Bicentennial Conference. Sir William Holford in *The Listener*, 16 June 1955, and *Journal of the R.I.B.A.*, 1958, p. 269 ff. On the developments of Paris in the 19th century, cf. D. H. Pinkney, *Napoleon III and the Rebuilding of Paris*, Princeton University Press, 1958. G. Shankland in *Architectural Association Journal*, 1957, pp. 149 ff. and 190 ff. See also the September number of *Architecture and Building*, 1958, containing a concise and thoughtful discussion of urban redevelopment, centred upon Boston Manor. On the opposite attitude, conservative in the true sense of the word, cf. S. Crowe, *To-morrow's Landscape*, London 1956.

22. Karl Marx, *Capital*, Vol. 1, Chicago 1915, pp. 25, 26 and 338.

23. cf. N. Pearson in *Planning Outlook*, 1957, p. 16 ff.

24. M. Holloway, op. cit. F. Tilsley's novel, *Champion Road*, London 1948, gives a telling description of the rise of the speculative builder in the north of England. cf. Lavedan III, p. 53 ff.

25. cf. B. M. Lane, *Architecture and Politics in Germany 1918–45*, Harvard University Press 1968; and A. Speer, *Inside the Third Reich*, London 1970.

26. K. Mannheim, *Ideology and Utopia*, London, numerous editions. *Social Purpose*, *passim*.

27. Sir William Holford in *Architectural* Review, December 1957, p. 394 ff.

28. K. Mannheim, *Diagnosis of Our Time*, London 1943, *passim*. cf. also the present writer in *Journal of the R.I.B.A.*, September 1961, p. 2 ff.

29. A. Aalto in *Journal of the R.I.B.A.*, May 1957, p. 258 ff.

30. On life in Bethnal Green as contrasted with a modern housing estate, described fictitiously as 'Greenleigh', cf. M. Young and P. Wilmott, *Family and Kinship in East London*, London 1957.

31. S. Kadleigh, *High Paddington*, London 1952.

32. K. Mannheim, op. cit., *passim*. Jane Jacobs, *The Death and Life of Great American Cities*, London 1962.

33. E. J. Mishan, *The Costs of Economic Growth*, Harmondsworth 1969, especially p. 131. cf. also J. K. Galbraith, *The Affluent Society*, Boston 1958, 2nd ed., London 1969.

34. *Goethe-Museum*, ed. H. Holtzhauer, Berlin and Weimar 1969. W. S. Heckscher in *Jahrbuch der Hamburger Kunstsammlungen*, Cen. VII, 1962, p. 35 ff.

35. J. M. Richards in *Architectural Review*, May 1958, p. 299 ff., on the 'false glamour' of the private motor-car.

36. C. Doxiadis, *Ekistics*, London 1968.

37. P. Soleri, *Arcology, The City in the Image of Man*, M.I.T. Press, Cambridge, Mass. 1969. H. Skolimowski in *Architectural Association Quarterly*, III, 1971, p. 35 ff.

38. The widening of feminine horizons and consciousness is clearly seen in Jane B. Drew, E. M. Fry and H. L. Ford, *Village Housing in the Tropics*, London 1947, the text of which was written, as Miss Drew kindly informs me, solely by herself. On woman's liberation, see Millett, op. cit., *passim*.

39. M. E. Spiro, *Kibbutz, Venture in Utopia*, Cambridge, Mass., 1956, especially pp. 125, 130 f.

40. Professor J. S. Passmore in *Philosophy*, April 1958, p. 109.

41. H. Read, *Anarchy and Order*, London 1954, p. 221 f.

42. *Citizen & City in the Year 2000*, published by The European Cultural Foundation, Deventer 1971.

CONCISE BIBLIOGRAPHY

For further references the notes should be consulted

I Sources

Manuscripts

Boullée, E.-L., *Architecture, Essai sur l'art*, Bibliothèque Nationale, Paris.

Dance, G., Material in the Sir John Soane's Museum and the Royal Institute of British Architects, London.

Filarete (A. Averlino), *Trattato d'Architettura*, numerous manuscripts, the most important being the *Codex Magliabecchianus*, Biblioteca Nazionale, Florence.

Leonardo da Vinci, Manuscript B of the Institut de France, Paris.

Missal of Pompeo Colonna, John Rylands Library, Manchester.

Printed Works

Adam, Robert and James, *The Works in Architecture*, London 1773–1782.

Alberti, L. B., *De Re Aedificatoria, libri decem*, written *c*. 1450; published in Latin in 1485, in Italian in 1546 and 1550, and in French in 1553.

Collection des prix que la ci-devant Académie d'Architecture proposoit et couronnoit tous les ans, 1787–96.

Dürer, A., *Etliche Underricht zu Befestigung der Stett, Schloss und flecken*, Nürnberg 1527.

Fourier, C., *Le Nouveau Monde*, Paris 1829.

Ledoux, C.-N., *L'Architecture considérée sous le rapport de l'art, des mœurs et de la législation*, Paris 1804–46.

Martini, Fr. di Giorgio, *Trattato di Architettura Civile e Militare*, especially Vol. III, about 1495; published in Turin in 1841.

Owen, R., *A New View of Society*, numerous editions.

Patte, P., *Monumens érigés à la gloire de Louis XV*, Paris 1765.

Poliphilo (Fr. Colonna), *Hypnerotomachia*, numerous editions.

Pugin, A. W. N., *Contrasts*, London 1836.

Scamozzi, V., *L'Idea della Architettura Universale*, Venice 1615.

Serlio, S., *Tutte l'Opere d'Architettura*, Venice 1584.

Vitruvius Pollio, *De Architectura, libri decem*, numerous illustrated editions, among which those of Joannes de Tridino of 1511 in Venice, Cesare Cesariano of 1521 in Como, the French version by Jean Martin of 1547 and the *Vitruvius Teutsch* of Rivius of 1548 are the most important.

II Monographs

Fels, Comte de, *Ange-Jacques Gabriel*, Paris 1924.

Hahnloser, H. R., *Villard de Honnecourt*, Vienna 1935.

Jordan, H., *Forma Urbis Romae*, Berlin 1874.

Lazzaroni, M. and Muñoz, A., *Filarete*, Rome 1908.

Le Corbusier, *Œuvre complète*, Zurich, numerous editions.

Oettingen, W. von, *Filarete's Tractat über die Baukunst*, Vienna 1890.

Réau, L., *Le Rayonnement de Paris au XVIIIe siècle*, Paris 1946.

Rosenau, H., *Boullée's Treatise on Architecture*, London 1953.

Weller, A. S., *Francesco di Giorgio*, Chicago 1943.

III Books for Reference

Bardet, G., *Naissance et méconnaissance de l'urbanisme*, Paris 1951.

Beresford, M., *New Towns of the Middle Ages*, London 1967.

Bowring, J., *The Works of J. Bentham*, Edinburgh 1843, etc.

Brinckmann, A. E., *Stadtbaukunst*, Berlin-Potsdam 1920.

Dickinson, R. E., The West European City, London 1951.

Dizionario Enciclopedico di Architettura e Urbanistica, Rome 1968–9, ed. P. Portognesi.

Doxiadis, C. A., *Ekistics*, London 1968.

Frankfort, H., *The Art and Architecture of the Ancient Orient*, Harmondsworth 1954.

Giedion, S., *Space, Time and Architecture*, 3rd ed., London 1954.

Hautecœur, L., *Histoire de l'architecture classique en France*, Paris 1943–53.

Heckscher, W. S., in *Jahrbuch der Hamburger Kunstsammlungen*, VII, 1962, p. 35 ff.

Hitchcock, H.-R., *Architecture, Nineteenth and Twentieth Centuries*, Harmondsworth 1958.

Howard, E., *Garden Cities of Tomorrow*, with a preface by F. J. Osborn and an introduction by L. Mumford, London 1946.

Jacob, G., *Mannheim Einst und Jetzt*, Mannheim 1959.

Jacobs, Jane, *Death and Life of Great American Cities*, London 1962.

Kaufmann, E., *Architecture in the Age of Reason*, Cambridge, Mass. 1955.

Kimball, F., *The Creation of the Rococo*, Philadelphia 1943.

Kopp, A., *Town and Revolution: Soviet Architecture and City Planning 1917–35*, London 1970.

Krinsky, C. H., *Journal of the Warburg and Courtauld Institutes*, 23, 1970, p. 1 ff.

Lampl, P., *Cities and Planning in the Ancient Near East*, New York 1968.

Lane, B. M., *Architecture and Politics in Germany*, Harvard University Press 1968.

Lavedan, P., *Histoire de l'urbanisme*, Paris 1926–52.

Lynch, Kevin, *The Image of the City*, Technology Press and Harvard University Press, Cambridge, Mass. 1960.

Mishan, E. J., *The Costs of Economic Growth*, Harmondsworth 1967.

Muehsam, A., *Coin and Temple*, Leeds University Press 1966.

Münter, G., *Idealstädte*, Berlin 1957.

Olivetti, Marco M., *Il Tempio Simbolo Cosmico*, Rome 1967.

Parrot, *Ziggurats et Tour de Babel*, Paris 1949.

Petrocchi, M., *Razionalismo architettonico e razionalismo storiografico*, Rome 1947.

Quatremère de Quincy, A.-C., (ed.), '*Architecture*', *Encyclopédie méthodique*, Paris 1785–1820.

Reps, J. W., *The Making of Urban America*, Princeton University Press 1965. *Monumental Washington*, Princeton University Press 1967. *Town Planning in Frontier Towns*, Princeton University Press 1969.

Rosenau, H., *Design and Medieval Architecture*, London 1934. *The Painter J.-L. David*, London 1948.

Soleri, P., *Arcology, The City in the Image of Man*, Massachusetts Institute of Technology Press 1969.

Speer, A., *Inside the Third Reich*, London 1970.

Stamm, R., (ed.), *Die Kunstformen des Barock-Zeitalters*, Berne 1956.

Stern, J., *A l'ombre de Sophie Arnould: F.-J. Bélanger, architecte des menus plaisirs*, Paris 1930.

Toy, S., *A History of Fortification*, London 1955.

Toynbee, A., *Cities on the Move*, London, 1970. *Cities of Destiny*, (ed.), London 1967.

Tunnard, Chr., *The City of Man*, London 1953.

Valdenaire, A., *Karlsruhe, die klassisch gebaute Stadt*, Augsburg 1929.

Wiebenson, D., *Tony Garnier: The Cité Industrielle*, New York 1969.

Wittkower, R., *Architectural Principles in the Age of Humanism*, 1st ed., London 1949.

Wycherley, R. E., *How the Greeks Built Cities*, London 1949.

Zeitler, R., *Klassizismus und Utopia*, Stockholm 1954.

INDEX